THE COLOSSIAN IMAGE

THE COLOSSIAN IMAGE

Paul's Vision for Renewed Humanity
and Life in Christ in Colossians

MANFRED P. HEDLEY

ALDERWAY PUBLISHING

First published in Great Britain in 2016

Alderway Publishing
(an imprint of Emblem Books)
Ashill, Norfolk
www.alderway.com

Copyright © Manfred P. Hedley 2016

All rights reserved. No part of this book may be reproduced or transmitted in any form or by any means, electronic or mechanical, including photocopying, recording, or by any information storage and retrieval system, except for brief quotations in critical reviews or articles, without permission in writing from the publisher.

Unless otherwise stated, biblical references are either the author's own translation or taken from the New Revised Standard Version of the Bible, Anglicized Edition, copyright © 1989, 1995 by the Division of Christian Education of the National Council of the Churches of Christ in the United States of America. Used by permission. All rights reserved.

British Library Cataloguing-in-Publication Data
A catalogue record for this book is available from the British Library

ISBN 978-1-908667-40-3

2 4 6 8 10 9 7 5 3 1

Printed and distributed by Lightning Source UK.

With love and thanks to Mum and Dad

CONTENTS

Preface		9
Abbreviations		17
List of figures and tables		19
Introduction: A new and true humanity		21

Part One: Humanity in Colossians

1	True humanity	41
2	Faith, hope, and love	49
3	Exemplified in Christ	61
4	Living a cruciform life	71
5	Sharing in resurrection	83

Part Two: The Image of God in Colossians

6	Christ, the image	95
7	Image and empire	105
8	Image and wisdom	117
9	Image and creation	123
10	Humanity, the image	137

Part Three: Life 'in Christ' in Colossians

11	Living 'in him'	147
12	The Colossian deception	155
13	Relocating law into Christ	167
14	Covenantal eikonism	183
15	Eikonic life in Christ	197

Bibliography of cited works		207
Index of ancient sources		223

PREFACE

In the beginning God created the heavens and the earth ... Then God said, "Let us create humanity in our image."

Genesis 1:1, 26

The book of Genesis is in many ways a book of introductions. At its beginning we know nothing of God; by its end we have met our Creator and already know Him well. At the beginning we know little about ourselves; by its end we understand the roots of our frailty, the devastation of sin, and yet also our capacity for faithfulness and fruitfulness. At its beginning we know nothing of God's purposes; by its end we have heard His call into covenant, His plan A for saving His people, and have watched the scene being set for His great work of salvation in Egypt. And of course, by the end of Genesis we have been introduced to so many of the key figures who inform or exemplify our understanding of living by faith: Adam, Abel, Noah, Abraham, Jacob, Joseph.

For all of these introductions throughout the book of Genesis, the most important are made on its first page. For it is Genesis 1 that we first meet God, who is introduced as the one, eternal, relational, powerful, life-giving Creator God, whose nature is revealed through His words and actions; and it is here that we first meet ourselves, humanity, and discover our God-given identity and purpose: to bear His image to the world.

Unpacking this image identity has formed a core part of my work as a theologian for a number of years, and is the starting point for much of the teaching we deliver at Fountain School of Theology in Norfolk, UK. Specifically, I have focused my attention on identifying the thematic framework established in Genesis 1, which gives the image of God definition and a language that can be traced throughout Scripture, such that it emerges as the golden seam that runs through the human narrative in both the OT and the NT, rarely at the surface but always influential, to reveal a coherent biblical metanarrative telling the rise, fall, and restoration of God's image in creation.

I have previously unpacked my interpretation of Genesis 1 and its implications for humanity in the book *The God of Page One: Rediscovering God's Identity and Ours* (Emblem Books, 2012), and have taught extensively on how I see this unfolding throughout the Old Testament and in the Gospels. However, a significant gap in the narrative picture I have previously drawn has been its influence on Paul's writing. This is largely the result of my natural inclinations both as an Old Testament theologian and an exegete of biblical narrative, but clearly Paul's influence on Christian theology is (rightly) so strong that he cannot be left out of any attempt to demonstrate a coherence to the whole biblical story.

Moreover, it is clear that Paul's understanding of the image of God is fundamental to his anthropology, since he draws it into the heart of his treatise of the redemption of Christ (Rom 8:29; 1 Cor 15:49; 2 Cor 3:8; 4:4). This is most distinct in his letter to the Colossians, in which he identifies Jesus as "the image of the invisible God" (Col 1:15) before showing how the Church has been "renewed in knowledge according to the image of its creator" (Col 3:10). This renewal is effected, says Paul, through a life lived 'in Christ', which enters into his death, shares in his resurrection, and displays the hallmarks of his love.

This being the case, I was delighted to be given the opportunity to study Paul's treatment of the image of God in Colossians as the research topic for my Master's degree in Kingdom Theology with Westminster Theological Centre, with a view to demonstrating a close correlation between my reading of Genesis and Paul's vision for life 'in Christ'. This book is the result of that research, and is essentially my dissertation, reprinted with some additions and corrections.

As such, contrary to the deliberately accessible tone of *The God of Page One*, this is an expressly academic study. The result, I hope, is a work of theological depth that builds firm foundations for my previous written work, and makes a helpful contribution to the academic debate about the true meaning and implications of humanity's creation in the image of God. I am thankful that the enthusiastic response I have had so far to this material, both academic and lay, suggests I may not be entirely on the wrong track.

Summary abstract

The purpose of this research is to examine the presentation of humanity in Paul's letter to the Colossians, specifically with regard to the language of the image of God (Col 1:15, 3:10) and life in Christ. My aim is to assess how far Colossians displays an anthropology rooted in the Genesis portrayal of the image of God, and whether this shapes Paul's understanding of Christian spirituality and lifestyle. Such a study is important because it seeks to develop a clearer picture of the high anthropology present in Colossians, which not only has implications for how the key themes of Christology and the Colossian crisis are understood, but also how Paul's view of the Law is shaped by his theology of the image of God.

The approach I have adopted is principally one of biblical exegesis rooted in the New Testament, with some significant reference to the Old Testament (especially Genesis 1), plus some typological, intertextual and historical critical analyses interwoven into the study. My findings are that true humanity is portrayed according to the same characteristics of indwelling relationship, authority, power and unity as the image of God in Genesis 1:26-28, and that they are established through participating in the death and resurrection of Christ. Moreover, that these same hallmarks are identified as integral to Paul's description of life 'in Christ.'

From this, we may conclude that Colossians displays a high anthropology, in which humans are re-created according to Christ's image identity. This challenges the view that Paul envisioned a Christian life built on the principles of 'covenantal nomism' – living by the Law in loving response to God's covenant initiative. Instead, he envisioned a life of 'covenantal eikonism' – living as the image of God in loving response to Christ's New Covenant initiative. I therefore recommend that Colossians should be read in terms of an 'advanced Christology', embracing both a high (divine) and low (human) understanding of Christ's identity, which serves to elevate humanity in its wake and offer a practical model for Christian life in the New Covenant.

Acknowledgements

There are several people to whom I am greatly indebted in the preparation and writing of this book. Firstly, I would like to express my huge gratitude to my dissertation supervisor, Dr Tony Cummins, for his time, advice, encouragement, challenge and correction. I have greatly valued his support, and have benefited so much from his wisdom and knowledge. He has kept me on track, and his input has consistently proved to be insightful and to inspire new (often essential) thoughts, which have lifted my writing and argument.

I also want to thank Dr Lucy Peppiatt and Dr Matthew Lynch, Principal and Dean of Studies respectively at Westminster Theological Centre, and both valued friends and colleagues, for their advice and encouragement, both in the early stages of honing the direction of my research and throughout the writing process. In addition, I am very grateful to the staff team at Westminster Theological Centre for allowing me access to their central library and giving me space in the office to carry out so much of my research. This put several invaluable sources into my hands, and offered a welcome and enjoyable tonic to the otherwise largely solitary process of research.

My sincere thanks also go to the team at Fountain School of Theology, whom I am privileged to lead, Fountain of Life Church, both as my employer and spiritual home, and Stephen Mawditt in particular, for their (and his) friendship, encouragement and enthusiasm, and the willingness to release so much of my time to my studies in general, and this research in particular.

Finally, I would like to thank my family: my wife Ali, our two children, my parents Miles and Charmaine, and our dear friends Rachel and Richard Kehoe, for their constant love, support, patience, adaptability, and belief in the value of what I was doing. More sacrifices have been made by each than is reasonable to try and summarise, and I am so thankful for you all.

Manfred P. Hedley, July 2016.

ABBREVIATIONS

Cf.	Conferre (compare with)
ESV	Holy Bible, English Standard Version
Fig.	Figure diagram
KJV	Holy Bible, King James Version
LXX	The Septuagint (Greek Old Testament)
NIV	Holy Bible, New International Version
NLT	Holy Bible, New Living Translation
NPNF	Nicene and Post-Nicene Fathers
NRSV	Holy Bible, New Revised Standard Version
NT	New Testament
OT	Old Testament
vv.	Verses (inclusive)

Old Testament Books

Gen	Genesis	Neh	Nehemiah
Ex	Exodus	Est	Esther
Lev	Leviticus	Ps	Psalms
Num	Numbers	Prov	Proverbs
Deut	Deuteronomy	Isa	Isaiah
Jos	Joshua	Jer	Jeremiah
Jdg	Judges	Eze	Ezekiel
1 Sam	1 Samuel	Dan	Daniel
2 Sam	2 Samuel	Hos	Hosea
1 Kgs	1 Kings	Am	Amos
2 Kgs	2 Kings	Mic	Micah
1 Chr	1 Chronicles	Zec	Zechariah
2 Chr	2 Chronicles		

OT Apocrypha

Wis	Wisdom of Solomon	Sir	Ben-Sirach
		2 Esd	2 Esdras

Pseudepigrapha

LAris	Letter of Aristeas	TAb	Testament of Abraham
2 Bar	2 Baruch		
3 Bar	3 Baruch	TLev	Testament of Levi
1 En	1 Enoch	TSol	Testament of Solomon
2 En	2 Enoch		
3 En	3 Enoch	4 Ez	4 Ezra

New Testament Books

Mt	Matthew	Col	Colossians
Mk	Mark	1 Thes	1 Thessalonians
Lk	Luke	2 Thes	2 Thessalonians
Jn	John	1 Tim	1 Timothy
Acts	Acts of the Apostles	2 Tim	2 Timothy
Rom	Romans	Tts	Titus
1 Cor	1 Corinthians	Phm	Philemon
2 Cor	2 Corinthians	Heb	Hebrews
Gal	Galatians	1 Pet	1 Peter
Eph	Ephesians	1 Jn	1 John
Phil	Philippians	Rev	Revelation

NT Apocrypha

CavTre Cave of Treasures

LIST OF FIGURES AND TABLES

Fig. A:	Advanced Christology	27
Fig. B:	Colossians 1:3-9 chiasmus	55
Fig. C:	Colossians 1:3-12 chiasmus	56
Fig. D:	Colossians 1:13-20 chiasmus	65
Fig. E:	Colossians 1:24-2:5 chiasmus	74
Fig. F:	Colossians 2:6-19 chiasmus	87
Fig. G:	Colossians 2:20-3:4 parallelism	89
Fig. H:	Colossians 3:5-17 chiasmus	90
Fig. I:	Colossians 1:13-20 chiasmus	101
Fig. J:	Tiberius denarius	108
Fig. K:	The image of God in creation	134
Fig. L:	Colossians 2:6-19 chiasmus	186
Tab. A:	Potential Gnostic, Mystic Influences	160
Tab. B:	Potential Hellenistic Influences	161

Introduction

A NEW AND TRUE HUMANITY

Pick up any commentary on Colossians and you will find a summary introduction giving an overview of the principal themes of the letter. Typically these are dominated by two overarching observations. First, that Paul is countering a crisis in Colossae (Col 2:8-23).[1] Second, that he does so by affirming the Christological supremacy of Jesus (1:13-23): his lordship over creation (1:15), his sovereignty over sin and evil, indeed all powers (1:16), and his liberation of God's people (1:13-14, 21-22).[2]

---

[1] See, for example, Dunn, *The Epistles to the Colossians and to Philemon*, 23; Wright, *Colossians and Philemon*, 25-26; Thompson, *Colossians and Philemon*, 6-7; Lincoln, *Colossians*, 568; Martin, *Colossians and Philemon*, 8-9.

[2] For Christ's supremacy generally, see Barclay, *Colossians and Philemon*, 77; Thompson, *Colossians and Philemon*, 11; Lincoln, *Colossians*, 568-69. For his lordship over creation, see Wright, *Colossians and Philemon*, 32; O'Brien, *Colossians, Philemon*, xl. For his sovereignty over sin, evil and all powers, see Lucas, *The Message of Colossians and Philemon*, 24; Wall, *Colossians and*

In emphasising these two aspects, commentators have sought succinctly to capture both the occasion and the prevailing theology of the letter. However, while there can be no doubting the vital importance of each, which certainly give the letter so much of its distinctive flavour, we must account for the fact that neither is a constant feature. In fact, while both dominate the first half of the letter (1:3-2:23), neither has any explicit bearing on the second half, where the focus shifts from conceptual to applied theology as Paul attends to a practical vision for Christian attitudes, lifestyle, and relationships (3:1-4:17).

The tendency has been to view this shift as addressing the implications of Christ's supremacy for the Church, and it certainly seems that Colossians 3:1-4 acts as a bridge to that effect: "If you have been raised with Christ..." (3:1) becomes the rationale for everything that follows. However, Paul's emphasis throughout chapters three and four is on the transformation the Colossians have received, not the divine power of Christ that caused it.

This transformation amounts to more than a list of improved behaviours, which afford an appropriate response to the sacrificial act and divine love of Christ. It

---

Philemon, 25-26; Lincoln, *Colossians*, 570; O'Brien, *Colossians, Philemon*, xxxviii; Thompson, *Colossians and Philemon*, 11-12. For his liberation of God's people, see Thompson, *Colossians and Philemon*, 12; Martin, *Colossians and Philemon*, 19.

A New and True Humanity

is a comprehensive re-imagination, even recreation, of humanity itself:

> Do not lie to one another, seeing that you have stripped off the old self with its practices and have clothed yourselves with the new self, which is being renewed in knowledge according to the image of its creator. In that renewal there is no longer Greek and Jew, circumcised and uncircumcised, barbarian, Scythian, slave and free; but Christ is all and in all!
> Colossians 3:9-11

That is not to side-line the primacy of Christ. In fact, Paul holds Christ at the heart of this transformation by connecting his identity as "the image of the invisible God" (Col 1:15) with humanity's renewal "according to the image of its creator" (3:10). In doing so, he correlates this renewed humanity with the supreme Christ, thereby separating humanity from the rest of creation.

Paul had already done this by describing Christ's primacy in creation ("in him all things on heaven and on earth were created," Col 1:16) and over the Church ("He is the head of the body, the church," Col 1:18) as independent expressions of authority, but now he presses his point further. After the cross, it is not only Christ who ascends, but all those who have become "true humanity" ascend with him:

> When you were buried with him in baptism, you were also raised with him through faith in the power of God, who raised him from the dead.
> Colossians 2:12

> So if you have been raised with Christ, seek the things that are above, where Christ is, seated at the right hand of God.
> Colossians 3:1

Thus the human narrative of creation-fall-recreation is brought to completion by Christ crucified, as humanity is remade according to the blueprint of the Creator, not the blueprint of creation.

This naturally provokes questions about how far Colossians reflects an anthropology of theosis. That is, in which humanity may attain to a level of divinisation. As Athanasius put it, "He was made man that we might be made God" (cf. 1 Cor 1:30; 2 Cor 5:21; 8:9).[3] It also points to a more fundamental understanding of the nature of

---

[3] Athanasius, *On The Incarnation Of The Word* 54.3. Translated in Athanasius, "On The Incarnation Of The Word," in *NPNF 2-04* 332.

A New and True Humanity

humanity in God's eyes. If there is a vision of theosis, or any scheme in which "true humanity" is to be understood according to Christ, then there must be an underlying assumption, or series of assumptions, about what constitutes true humanity. How do we as humans "live and move and have our being" (Acts 17:28)?

While Paul's catch-all answer to this is "in him" (Col 2:6, 7, 9, 10, 11, 12), he gives us certain markers that may give substance to this assurance. True humanity shares the fullness that is to be found in Christ (2:10 cf. 1:19; 2:9), bears the authority that belongs to Christ (2:10 cf. 1:16; 2:15), and enters into the same power of life over death as Christ (2:12 cf. 1:18). Drawing these threads together, Paul declares that true humanity is "renewed in knowledge according to the image of its creator" (3:10), just as Christ is "the image of the invisible God" (1:15). This neatly sums up the human story that lies behind the dominant Christological themes of the letter, a story that moves from sinful to saved, distant to reconciled, broken to renewed.

The key, therefore, is understanding Paul's use of the image of God in Colossians. By identifying Jesus as the image, is Paul asserting Christ's divinity, as he alone looks exactly like God (cf. Jn 14:9), having participated in creation (Col 1:16) and borne God's authority (1:17), because the fullness of God dwells within him (1:19)? In which case, any alignment between humanity and *that* image would seem highly theotic.

Conversely, is it a statement of Christ's humanity, as he alone perfectly embodies the prototype for humans in creation, made in the image of God (cf. Gen 1:26-27)? Or, considering the prevalence of iconography used within the Roman imperial cult to portray the deification of the emperor, could it be a proclamation of Christ's lordship over all pretenders, thereby challenging the authority of Rome and the perverted vision of divine authority conveyed on Caesar?[4]

I believe Paul intends all three to be read, and that while there is certainly a distinctly 'high Christology' (emphasising Christ's divinity) at work, especially in the so-called "Christ hymn" (Col 1:15-20), we dismiss the parallel 'low Christology' (emphasising Christ's humanity) at our peril. For when we do, we underestimate the importance of Paul's anthropological argument throughout Colossians.

It is perhaps better, then, to speak of an 'advanced Christology,' encapsulating both high and low, which serves to confirm not only Christ's divinity and supremacy over all powers in creation, but also his primacy in the emergence of a new humanity, created

---

[4] For an overview of the use of iconography within the imperial cult, including on coins, monuments, statues and inscriptions, see Gorman, *Apostle of the Crucified Lord*, 15-18.

through participation in him (cf. e.g., Col 2:6-7; 3:9-11), which in turn establishes his lordship when both are held together (see Fig. A).

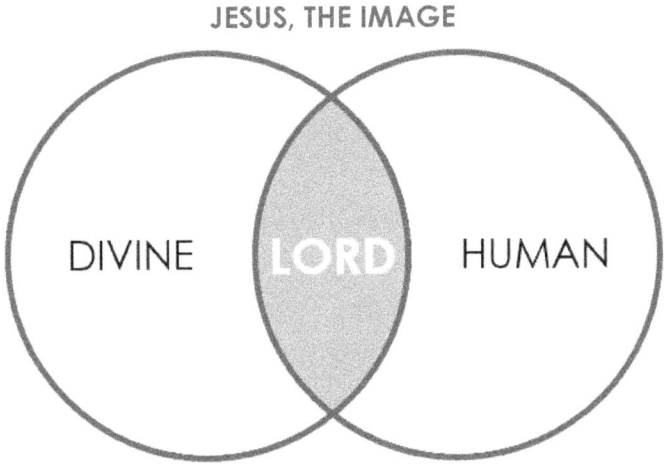

Fig. A – Advanced Christology

In this short book, I want to argue that Paul's vision for Christ's image-bearing identity being inherited by humanity constitutes a transposition from an 'advanced Christology' to a 'high anthropology,' which underpins the motivation and theology of the letter as a whole.

The Colossian Image

Positioning the study

The presence of humanity as a theme in Paul's argument has not gone unnoticed by interpreters,[5] but compared with the obvious importance of the dominant themes of crisis and Christology, it has tended to fade into the background. It is notable that several influential commentaries omit any in-depth anthropological analysis in their theological summaries of the letter,[6] while those who do usually fail to develop their assertions beyond a few passing remarks. Consequently, this remains a largely underdeveloped area of study. Nevertheless, a number of important observations have been made regarding the nature of humanity in Colossians.

Several commentators have pointed to Colossians 3:9-11 as the start of a "new humanity,"[7] which has been defined ontologically by Douglas Moo as the "total reorientation of one's existence."[8] Michael Gorman has discussed this in

---

[5] Barclay (*Colossians and Philemon*, 87), Thompson (*Colossians and Philemon*, 11), Martin (*Colossians and Philemon*, 22) and Lincoln (*Colossians*, 570-71) all stand as important examples.
[6] See Dunn, *Colossians and Philemon*, 19-41; O'Brien, *Colossians, Philemon*, xxvi-liv; Thompson, *Colossians and Philemon*, 1-12; Wall, *Colossians and Philemon*, 13-29.
[7] See Patzia, *Ephesians, Colossians, Philemon*, 76; Lincoln, *Colossians*, 574-75; Dunn, *Colossians and Philemon*, 121; Martin, *Colossians and Philemon*, 22; Thompson, *Colossians and Philemon*, 78.
[8] Moo, *Colossians and Philemon*, 77.

terms of a process of theosis,[9] whereas others have maintained a clear division between humanity and divinity. John Barclay, for example, sees "humanity as it was designed to be, humanity at its fullest and highest potential."[10] N. T. Wright in turn speaks of "true humanity," whose "standard is now the life of heaven."[11] The connection being made, of course, is to Genesis 1:26-28, where humanity's highest potential as the image of God is first depicted.[12] There is, clearly, also a connection made with Colossians 1:15, where Christ is likewise identified as "the image [εἰκων, eikon] of the invisible God." As Douglas Moo puts it, "Christ supplies the pattern for the renewal of the 'new self'" (cf. Rom 8:29).[13]

At one level, this dual connection surrounding Paul's use of εἰκων has led to a rich discussion about how the Church receives this new identity. Paul's depiction of the Church

---

[9] Gorman, *Inhabiting the Cruciform God*, 90-93.
[10] Barclay, *Colossians and Philemon*, 87; cf. Thompson, *Colossians and Philemon*, 46.
[11] Wright, *Colossians and Philemon*, 142; cf. Thiselton, *The Living Paul*, 67.
[12] E.g., Dunn, *Colossians and Philemon*, 222; Martin, *Colossians and Philemon*, 107; Beetham, *Echoes of Scripture*, 241; Sumney, "Writing "In The Image" Of Scripture," in *Paul and Scripture: Extending the Conversation* 210; O'Brien, *Colossians, Philemon*, 191; Fee, *Pauline Christology*, 303; Thompson, *Colossians and Philemon*, 78; Moo, *Colossians and Philemon*, 269.
[13] Moo, *Colossians and Philemon*, 270.

sharing in the death and resurrection of Christ (Col 2:12, 20; 3:1) has provided the backbone for this discussion, with many interpreters describing Christian transformation as the result of participation with Christ.[14] Whereas most will point to baptism as being at the forefront of Paul's mind here,[15] the importance of a daily adoption of Christlikeness, sharing in his afflictions (Col 1:24) and reflecting his lifestyle (3:5-17), has also been widely asserted, perhaps most notably by Michael Gorman as he has argued that Paul envisions the Christian life as one of cruciformity, which he defines as "participatory holiness."[16]

However, although the connection between Colossians 3:10 and Genesis 1:26-28 is widely accepted, the same cannot be said of Colossians 1:15. While it is broadly acknowledged that Paul echoes humanity's image identity in Genesis 1,[17] there is far less certainty that this connection is the primary intention. Essentially, the

---

[14] E.g., Thompson, *Colossians and Philemon*, 45; Dunn, *Colossians and Philemon*, 116, 161; Wright, *Colossians and Philemon*, 101,113; Wall, *Colossians and Philemon*, 115; O'Brien, *Colossians, Philemon*, 120.

[15] E.g., Barclay, *Colossians and Philemon*, 87,110; Dunn, *Colossians and Philemon*, 160; Connell, "Clothing the Body of Christ," *Worship* 135.

[16] Gorman, *Inhabiting the Cruciform God*, 115. For an overview of cruciformity in Paul, see Gorman, *Reading Paul*, 146-47.

[17] Thompson, *Colossians and Philemon*, 28-29; O'Brien, *Colossians, Philemon*, 43.

A New and True Humanity

debate surrounds how εἰκων would have been received by the letter's Colossian readers. For a church populated largely by Gentiles, in a Hellenistic context, εἰκων may arguably carry alternative connotations.[18]

Of the various proposals, two stand out. First, that Paul is actually correlating Jesus with the figure of Wisdom, who is depicted as a divine participant in creation in Proverbs 8:22-31 and described in relation to God as "an image of his goodness" (Wis 7:26).[19] Second, that Paul is challenging the Roman Empire – indeed any earthly authority - by contrasting the lordship of Christ with that of Caesar, who is proclaimed in Rome as the image of God.[20] Such a disagreement over Colossians 1:15 clearly has ramifications for our understanding of Colossians 3:10. If Colossians 1:15 presents Christ as divine, then humanity is called to reflect him. If Christ is lord, then humanity is called to represent him. But if he is human,

---

[18] For a brief overview of the Gentile dominance in the Colossian church, see O'Brien, *Colossians, Philemon*, xxviii-xxix.

[19] Cf. Barclay, *Colossians and Philemon*, 67; Wright, *Colossians and Philemon*, 71-72; O'Brien, *Colossians, Philemon*, 43; Dunn, *Colossians and Philemon*, 86-90; Lincoln, *Colossians*, 597; Thompson, *Colossians and Philemon*, 29; Wall, *Colossians and Philemon*, 66-67; Moo, *Colossians and Philemon*, 118-20.

[20] Horsley, *Paul and Empire*, 140; Walsh and Keesmaat, *Colossians Remixed*, 66, 89; Wright, *Paul: Fresh Perspectives*, 69.

then humanity is called to resonate him, even to become him.

Thus far, the debate has largely surrounded which of these three implications is correct. However, as I have stated above, I believe that all are consciously in play. Moreover, whatever conclusions have been drawn, the commitment to emphasise the high Christology has stifled any in-depth analysis of humanity in Colossians outside of Colossians 3:9-11, as interpreters have distanced themselves from a portrayal of Christ as the prototypical human and necessarily adopted a view of life "in Christ" that emphasises who we reflect over what we become.

Part of the problem has been the weight that has been attributed to a lexical study of εἰκων. Clearly this is an essential task to undertake, but as I have observed above, the letter as a whole moves beyond merely ascribing a title to humanity's renewal ("Image") by showing the actions and attributes that are associated with it, in order to depict how this new humanity is expressed in Christian life. Thus any interpretation of εἰκων must be in the context of how an "eikonic" life is described.

I will argue in this book that these actions and attributes may be summarised as four hallmarks of true humanity: i) sharing an intimate relationship of indwelling with God; ii) bearing His authority; iii) entering into His life-giving power; and iv) standing in unity. These hallmarks have been recognised with regard to Christ,[21] but studies exploring their relationship to humanity are lacking. The focus of this study is to examine these themes to see how they come together to reveal a vision for humanity that is rooted in Paul's convictions regarding God's original creation of the image of God, and the role of Christ not only in the restoration but the re-creation of this divinely-appointed human identity.

Parameters of the study

Any voyage through Colossians will naturally and necessarily enter some difficult waters, as contentious issues such as authorship and the Colossian crisis break against deconstructions of the letter's literary interpolations and complexities of translation.[22] The issues at play in each case are so fundamental to the letter that they can hardly be avoided, but they also carry the danger that one may drift without careful navigation. It is

---

[21] E.g., Indwelling: Wright, *Colossians and Philemon*, 80; authority: Lincoln, *Colossians*, 623; life-giving power: Gorman, *Apostle of the Crucified Lord*, 486; unity: Moo, *Colossians and Philemon*, 125-26.

[22] Consider, for example, Colossians 1:24 or 2:18, and the number of differing and conflicting translations and interpretations that have been offered in each case. We will visit each briefly later in this study.

important, therefore, that we keep the focus of this study in view.

This may be summarised into the following research question: How does Paul's presentation of humanity in the book of Colossians indicate an anthropology rooted in the Genesis portrayal of the image of God, and how does this shape his understanding of what it means to live a new life in Christ? In order to answer this question, I will examine Colossians closely, paying particular attention to its literary structure and how distinct units of composition interrelate to form a coherent argument, in which Christology and anthropology are discussed side by side. A careful analysis of Genesis 1:26-28 will also be necessary, not only to assess the use of "image" (צֶלֶם, *tselem*) but to see how the image of God is described in context. Alongside this, we will also reflect on a number of key texts from the Wisdom tradition, most notably Proverbs 8 and Wisdom of Solomon 7.

Taken as a whole, this is a work of biblical exegesis rooted in the New Testament. However, at its core there is also a significant typological (connecting Christ to the image of God figure) and intertextual argument to be made (connecting the theology of Colossians with that of the Jewish creation narrative). At the same time, a degree of historical criticism is necessary in order to understand how the theological implications connect with the first century Colossian and Jewish world.

A New and True Humanity

I am proceeding on the basis that Paul is the author of Colossians and will therefore refer to Paul throughout;[23] however, my argument neither hinges on "proving" such nor precludes fruitful correlation with other letters in the Pauline corpus. Nevertheless, I do believe that the argument put forth in this study is consistent with Paul's Christology and anthropology elsewhere. Therefore, while there is no space in this study to examine this in detail, I will offer cross-references to Paul's similar arguments elsewhere wherever possible, in the hope that it may justify further research.

Précis of the study

With all of this in mind, I will present my argument through the following three parts:

Part One: Humanity in Colossians.

In this part I will follow the letter through its whole argument in order to assess how humanity is presented, both in terms of its nature and its behaviour. By identifying a literary structure of discreet, often chiastic units, these chapters will also offer a lens into identifying the priorities of the letter, which come together to portray

---

[23] In line with Moo, *Colossians and Philemon*, 40; Wright, *Colossians and Philemon*, 36-37; O'Brien, *Colossians, Philemon*, xlix. Contrary to Dunn, *Colossians and Philemon*, 35; Lincoln, *Colossians*, 580.

an intimate relationship between the image-bearing identity of Christ and the renewal of humanity into that same image.

Part Two: The Image of God in Colossians.

This part will examine how Colossians uses "image of God" language to create a framework on which new humanity is constructed. I will analyse three possible interpretations of εἰκων to argue that Colossians draws on established Creation and Wisdom theology, consciously laced with anti-imperial overtones, in its presentation of Christ and the new humanity he creates. Essential to this analysis is a careful reading of Genesis 1:26-28 to compare the presentation of the image of God in creation with that discussed throughout Part One.

Part Three: Life 'in Christ' in Colossians.

This part will reflect on how Paul envisions this new humanity living "in Christ," both as a spiritual and a practical reality. Key to this analysis will be a discussion of the so-called 'Colossian heresy', which emerges most clearly within Paul's "in him" treatise. I will argue that Paul's emphasis on Christ over alternative influences, both Jewish and pagan, marks the entry into a process of transformation that results in a new humanity characterised by living according to the 'eikonic' blessings described in Genesis 1:26-28. Contrary to the arguments of E. P. Sanders and others for Paul's belief in 'covenantal nomism', this new lifestyle may be understood in terms of 'covenantal eikonism'. Finally, this part will close the study as a whole with a chapter in which I will revisit the conclusions drawn throughout to show how they overlap and interrelate to form one coherent vision for humanity that underpins the theological arguments in play throughout the epistle. Having done so, I will also reflect on the importance of the study and identify potential areas of further research.

PART ONE

Humanity in Colossians

There is no longer Greek and Jew, circumcised and uncircumcised, barbarian, Scythian, slave and free; but Christ is all and in all!

Colossians 3:11

Chapter One

TRUE HUMANITY

Colossians 1:1-2

Colossians is variously discussed with regards to its Christology, cosmology, eschatology, and ecclesiology,[24] but there is also a clear yet neglected anthropology that runs throughout the letter. Having expounded the supremacy of Christ (Col 1:15-20), Paul expresses his desire to present "every human" (πάντα ἄωθρωπον, panta anthropon, translation mine) as "mature in Christ" (Col 1:28). He then sets up "human tradition" (παράδοσιν τῶν ἀνθρώπων, paradosin ton anthropon) against Christ as opposing ethical standards (Col 2:8), which he goes on to describe as the difference between "the old humanity" (τὸν παλαιὸν ἄνθρωπον, ton palaion anthropon, Col 3:9) and "the new" (τὸν νέον, ton neon, Col 3:10).

---

[24] Helpful summaries of these themes are offered by Marianne Meye Thompson (Thompson, *Colossians and Philemon*, 10-11); cf. O'Brien, *Colossians, Philemon*, xlv-xlvi.

While the focus throughout is on the transformative influence of Christ, the human story is where that influence is proven, culminating in the emergence of a new humanity. This perspective is reinforced by Paul's frequent references to people, whether as named individuals or in terms of generic ethnic and societal people groups, which point to both the personal and comprehensive nature of this transformation.

At a community-wide level, this is apparent in the allusions to the cultural and ethnic make-up of the Colossian fellowship. Paul's reference to the Jews in his entourage (Aristarchus, Mark, Justus, 4:10-11), in addition to his assertion of "the riches of glory" revealed to the Gentiles (1:27), and the apparent mixture of Jewish and pagan rituals he criticised (2:8-23), all serve to indicate that the Colossian church was a community of Jews and Gentiles living and worshipping together, extending the relevance of Paul's message beyond Jewish boundaries. Moreover, the Haustafel references to wives and husbands (3:18-19), children and fathers (3:20-21), slaves and masters (3:22, 23; 4:1), as well as the extensive list of people groups in Colossians 3:11 ("Greek and Jew, circumcised and uncircumcised, barbarian, Scythian, slave and free"), further emphasise the comprehensive scope of the gospel to all humanity.

At a personal level, it is a common feature of Pauline epistles to call attention to specific individuals within the

True Humanity

Christian community as examples to follow or reject. Where Colossians stands out, however, is in the concentration of these examples in so short a text. Beyond the usual greetings, including Timothy (1:1), Luke and Demas (4:14), the Laodiceans (2:1; 4:3, 16), those in Hierapolis (4:13), Nympha and the church in her house (4:15), and Archippus (4:17), Paul specifically heralds Epaphras (1:7-8; 4:12), Tychius (4:7), and Onesimus (4:9) for their faithfulness, who themselves stand in juxtaposition to the Colossians as "faithful brothers" (πιστοῖς ἀδελφοῖς, pistois adelphois, Col 1:2), thereby drawing a direct connection between them.

Paul also offers himself as an example of a life which participates with Christ (1:24-2:5), and while much of the treatment of Jesus reflects a high Christology, it is important that we do not underplay significant references to the humanity of Jesus, who dies and stands as the firstborn of the new humanity in resurrection (1:18; 2:12). Indeed, it is this aspect of Christ that forms the basis of Paul's plea to the Colossians to live as Christ lived (3:1-4, 12-17).

Crucial to Paul's anthropology, then, is how it is expressed in the lives of faithful humans, living according to Christ (2:8), as a mark of their renewed humanity (3:10). With this in mind, over the next few chapters I intend to examine Colossians for what it has to say about the qualities of humanity, as exemplified in Christ and exhibited by his church. As we will see, Paul identifies four key hallmarks that characterise both: an intimate relationship with God, bearing authority, life-giving power, and unity.

Our navigational guide throughout this investigation will be to follow the delineation of literary units, which are often chiastic in nature, emphasising a central point from which the surrounding statements emanate and mirror one another. These units punctuate the letter to give it a defined anthropological framework, in which a clear distinction is drawn between humanity as it has existed up to Christ ("the old self," Col 3:9), and true humanity in light of Christ's life, death and resurrection ("the new self," Col 3:10). This true humanity, founded on faith, hope and love, is exemplified by Christ, and is thus entered into by participation with Christ, resulting in Christlikeness.

Introducing the concept

Paul begins with a description of the church as "the saints and faithful brothers and sisters in Christ in Colossae" (Col 1:2). In so doing, Paul characterises his audience as bearing three identifying marks.[25] First, they are 'saints'. While this certainly denotes holiness, it is principally Paul's usual greeting for the church (e.g., Rom 1:7; 1 Cor

---

[25] Cf. Thompson, *Colossians and Philemon*, 14.

1:2; 2 Cor 1:1; Phil 1:1; Eph 1:1).[26] But this is no small claim. Indeed, his use of ἅγιος (agios, which may denote a saint, or something holy) may evoke God's proclamation over Israel that "you shall be for me ... a holy nation" (Ex 19:6).[27]

For Paul, being a saint is akin to membership of God's holy people. This is reinforced by the second identifier, that they are 'faithful brothers and sisters'. Here again we find a covenantal allusion, this time to Israel's status as the chosen family of God (e.g., Am 3:1; Mic 2:3), and a nation founded on ἀδελφοί (adelphoi, brothers; e.g., Gen 47:11, LXX). Within this scheme, the faithfulness on display suggests a two-way relationship. In response to God choosing them to share in the New Covenant (cf. 1 Cor 11:25), they have chosen God by believing in Jesus, as they hold fast to one another in unity.

Finally, they are 'in Christ'. Standing in parallel to 'in Colossae',[28] this indicates a radical shift of identity, no longer shaped by the culture and climate of the world but by the character and cause of Christ.[29] Michael Gorman

---

[26] Barth and Blanke, *Colossians*, 139.
[27] Rendered ἔθνος ἅγιον (ethnos agion, holy people) in LXX (cf. Lev 19:2, again using ἅγιος in LXX).
[28] Wright notes that the structure of Colossians 1:2 balances ἐν Κολοσσαῖς (en Kolossais) and ἐν Χριστῷ (en Christo) either side of ἁγίοις καὶ πιστοῖς ἀδελφοῖς (agiois kai pistois adelphois): Wright, *Colossians and Philemon*, 50.
[29] Wright, *Colossians and Philemon*, 50; Moo, *Colossians and Philemon*, 77.

describes this as a "participatory holiness," in which Christians "inhabit God."[30] In other words, this is more than a mystical realignment of beliefs and priorities; it is a spiritual, social and ethical transformation that encompasses the whole of life. James Dunn calls this integration,[31] whereas Douglas Moo asserts it involves "total reorientation of one's existence."[32] For Paul, living 'in Christ' does not only mean becoming the "true people of God";[33] it also means integrating with and reflecting the true person of God. This, in particular, is a theme that Paul explicates in the main body of the letter to come (Col 2:6-4:1).

Together, these three identifiers provide an early indication of Paul's vision for what N. T. Wright terms "true humanity,"[34] at the heart of which is a reliance on and reflection of Christ, through whom humanity enjoys an intimate relationship with God, in which each has chosen the other. As Robert Wall puts it: "God's grace positions the *holy and faithful* community *in Christ* to participate in the glorious results of his messianic work."[35]

---

[30] Gorman, *Inhabiting the Cruciform God*, 115.
[31] Dunn, *Colossians and Philemon*, 50.
[32] Moo, *Colossians and Philemon*, 77.
[33] Wright, *Colossians and Philemon*, 50.
[34] Wright, *Colossians and Philemon*, 30; cf. Barclay, *Colossians and Philemon*, 87.
[35] Wall, *Colossians and Philemon*, 37.

True Humanity

The fact that Paul attributes these qualities to a community he appears later to criticise precisely for its questionable faithfulness to Christ (Col 2:6-23), suggests this is an ideal that Paul is holding forth, into which he is inviting the Colossians to mature (cf. 1:28).[36] In doing so, he sets the tone for everything that follows. As he proceeds to commend and convict them, what emerges is a picture of true humanity that displays the hallmarks of Christocentric life hinted at in his greeting.

---

[36] Cf. Thompson, *Colossians and Philemon*, 14.

Chapter Two

FAITH, HOPE, AND LOVE

Colossians 1:3-12

It would be easy to dismiss the thanksgiving in Colossians 1:3-12a merely as an extension of the greeting it follows, consistent with epistolary conventions in the ancient world,[37] and typical of Pauline literature (Rom 1:8f; 1 Cor 1:4f; Eph 1:15f; Phil 1:3f; 1 Thes 1:2f; 2 Thes 1:3f; 1 Tim 1:12f; 2 Tim 1:3-7; Phm 4f). However, it is well noted that Paul uses this standard form to foreshadow themes he wishes to discuss in the rest of the letter.[38]

---

[37] Dunn, *Colossians and Philemon*, 55; Wall, *Colossians and Philemon*, 39.
[38] See, for example, Kruse, *2 Corinthians*, 60; Moo, *The Epistle to the Romans*, 56; O'Brien, *Colossians, Philemon*, 7-8. For how this is displayed in Colossians specifically, see Garland, *Colossians and Philemon*, 44; Wright, *Colossians and Philemon*, 53; cf. Lincoln's alternative assertion that "its primary function is to assure the readers of the writer's goodwill toward them and his appreciation of the qualities of their Christian faith: Lincoln, *Colossians*, 590.

The Colossian Image

Among the various themes to be identified by commentators, including the typical Pauline emphasis on grace,[39] the truth and impact of the gospel,[40] and even possible allusions to a spiritual crisis within the community,[41] John Barclay notes the importance of thanksgiving itself, which he identifies as a repeated theme throughout the letter (Col 1:3, 12; 2:7; 3:15, 16, 17; 4:2)[42] and describes as "a central activity of this renewed humanity."[43]

This resonates with Robert Wall's assessment that thankfulness is an activity of covenantal fidelity, which demonstrates the depth of relationship between God and His people.[44] It is therefore significant that Paul starts by giving thanks (Col 1:3), expressing the covenantal relationship he holds, and then invites the Colossians to do the same (Col 1:12):

> May you be prepared to endure everything with patience, while joyfully giving thanks to the Father.
> Colossians 1:11-12

---

[39] Wright, *Colossians and Philemon*, 53; Martin, *Colossians and Philemon*, 49.
[40] Garland, *Colossians and Philemon*, 45; Moo, *Colossians and Philemon*, 86; Lucas, *The Message of Colossians and Philemon*, 27.
[41] Wall, *Colossians and Philemon*, 40.
[42] Cf. Garland, *Colossians and Philemon*, 47.
[43] Barclay, *Colossians and Philemon*, 88.
[44] Wall, *Colossians and Philemon*, 43.

Faith, Hope, and Love

This is the first of three subtle allusions in this thanksgiving to aspects of true humanity exemplified by others, each of which will be revisited at a later point in the letter. After the apostle himself (Col 1:3 cf. 1:23-2:5),[45] Paul lifts before them Jesus as their Lord (Col 1:3 cf. 1:15-20) and Epaphras as a "faithful minister of Christ on your behalf" (Col 1:7 cf. 4:12).

Of course, Paul's emphasis on the example of Christ is more than a standard to aspire to, and the high Christology that runs throughout the letter, with the soteriological implications this carries, has rightly dominated commentators' attention as the key theme in Paul's thanksgiving.[46] While the importance of Jesus as a model of human life is well-established[47] and remains an important subtext here, it is the absolute supremacy of Christ on which Paul relies. Perhaps the first hint of this supremacy comes with Paul's inclusion of Jesus alongside God as the catalyst for his thankfulness:

---

[45] While it is tempting to include Timothy in this example, noting Paul's use of the plural "In *our* prayers for you *we*..." (Col 1:3, italics mine) as a potential reference to Timothy as co-author of the letter, it is clear that Paul only offers himself as an example of Christ-like living later in the letter.

[46] Barclay, *Colossians and Philemon*, 79-80; Dunn, *Colossians and Philemon*, 55-56; Moo, *Colossians and Philemon*, 83.

[47] E.g., Gorman, *Reading Paul*, 129-130; Hooker, *Paul: A Short Introduction*, 106-107; Wenham, *Paul: Follower of Jesus or Founder of Christianity?*, 354-57.

The Colossian Image

> In our prayers for you we always thank God, the Father of our Lord Jesus Christ.
>
> Colossians 1:3

This is far from a consistent feature of Pauline letter-writing, with a number of his letters pointing only to God in its thanksgiving passages (Phil 1:3; 2 Thes 1:3; 2 Tim 1:3; Phm 4), but it is equally far from being unique to Colossians. Romans (1:8), 1 Corinthians (1:4), and 1 Thessalonians (1:2-3) all incorporate Jesus into Paul's thanks to God, whereas in 2 Corinthians and Ephesians Paul impresses upon his readers the familial unity between God and Christ, offering in turn the same scope of revelation as he does to the church in Colossae:

> Blessed be the God and Father of our Lord Jesus Christ.
>
> 2 Corinthians 1:3; Ephesians 1:3

The exact replication of these two passages (both εὐλογητὸς ὁ θεὸς καὶ πατὴρ τοῦ κυρίου ἡμῶν Ἰησοῦ Χριστοῦ, eulogetos o theos kai pater tou kyrion emon Iesou Christou), alongside the close correlation with Colossians 1:3 (εὐχαριστοῦμεν τῷ θεῷ πατρὶ τοῦ κυρίου ἡμῶν Ἰησοῦ Χριστοῦ, eucharistoumen to theo patri tou kyrion emon Iesou Christou) has led some to conclude that this designation

Faith, Hope, and Love

is drawn from the worship liturgy of the early church.[48] In which case, we find that from very early in the life of the church, Jesus was acclaimed by three qualifications: God is his father, he is Lord, and he is Christ.

In each case, what is emphasised is his pre-eminence on the basis of his relationship to God.[49] As God's Son he operates both as *divine ambassador* (i.e. κύριος, the term given for Yahweh in both the NT and the LXX),[50] and *human agent*, fulfilling God's vision for humanity in his messianic activity. Indeed, the correlation between the sonship of Jesus ("God, the Father of our Lord Jesus Christ," Col 1:3) and that of the Colossians ("God, *our* Father," Col 1:2, emphasis mine) serves to elevate all Christians, including Gentiles, to the exclusive covenantal promises previously reserved for Israel (Ex 4:22; Deut 32:6; Jer 3:9 cf. Jn 8:41).[51] Thus, as Christians enter into life 'in Christ,' exalting him as Lord and emulating him as the perfect human, they assume the covenantal identity of

---

[48] E.g. O'Brien, *Colossians, Philemon*, 10; Barth and Blanke, *Colossians*, 150.

[49] Moo, *Colossians and Philemon*, 83; O'Brien, *Colossians, Philemon*, 10; Lincoln, *Colossians*, 590.

[50] For NT, see, for example: Mt 1:22; Lk 1:68; Jn 12:13; Rom 9:29; Acts 3:22; Rev 4:8. For the LXX, see, for example: Gen 2:15; Ex 20:2; 1 Chr 11:9; Isa 40:3.

[51] Dunn, *Colossians and Philemon*, 55; Wright, *Colossians and Philemon*, 54; Martin, *Colossians and Philemon*, 47; Thompson, *Colossians and Philemon*, 19.

God's people, bringing with it the benefits of God's favour, including the Abrahamic commission to bless "all the families of the earth" (Gen 12:3). In this sense, they share in the authority and the agency of Christ.

Paul's invitation to see Epaphras as an exemplar of true humanity comes to the fore as we pay attention to the literary structure of the thanksgiving. Several commentators have noticed a chiastic structure, although there is some disagreement as to the parameters of this chiasmus. James Dunn and David Garland both identify vv.3-9 as a concentric unit, in which an inclusio is formed by the repeated assertion of Paul's constant prayer (1:3, 9).[52] This pinpoints v.6a as the vertex, emphasising the centrality of the gospel in Paul's message (see Fig. B).

The pattern they suggest is compelling, but it also has the negative effect of taking away from the unity of vv.9-11. Eduard Lohse has argued persuasively that the notable repetition of several terms between vv.3-8 and vv.9-12, including "since the day" (vv.6, 9), "we heard" (vv.4, 9), "bear fruit" (vv.6, 10), "giving thanks" (vv.3, 12), and "the saints" (vv.4, 12), points to a clear two-strophe structure, in which the second reflects the themes from the first.[53]

---

[52] Dunn, *Colossians and Philemon*, 54; Garland, *Colossians and Philemon*, 44-45.
[53] Lohse, *Colossians and Philemon*, 24. See also O'Brien, *Colossians, Philemon*, 18-19.

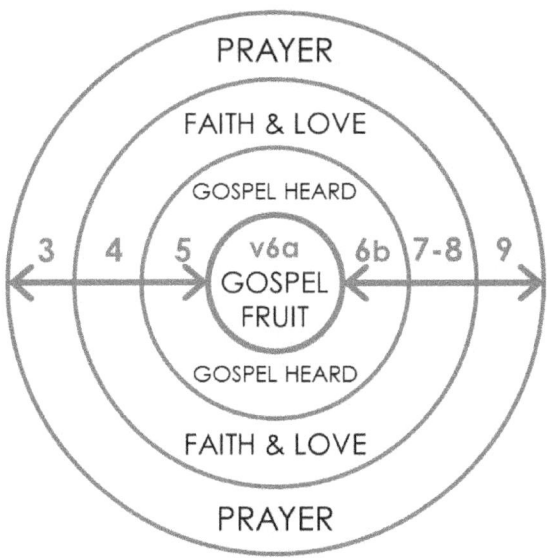

Fig. B – Colossians 1:3-9 chiasmus

Robert Wall has developed this thought by identifying a more extensive chiasmus (depicted in Fig. C, overleaf), which is framed within a different inclusio, delineated by the verb εὐχαριστέω (eucharisteo, "give thanks," 1:3, 12).[54] This fits neatly within Lohse's two-strophe scheme and corresponds with the emphasis on covenantal thanksgiving we noted above, and so is to be preferred over Dunn and Garland's proposal. Here the vertex shifts to the commendation of Epaphras (vv.7-8) who, like Paul

---

[54] Wall, *Colossians and Philemon*, 40-42; cf. Moo, *Colossians and Philemon*, 81.

the apostle (1:1) and Jesus the Lord and Messiah (1:3) is given titles that confirm his authority and agency: he is a "faithful minister" and a "fellow servant" (1:7). Within the Colossians' own community, they have known one who lives a life "worthy of the Lord" (1:10), and who has testified to the work of the Spirit alive in the whole Colossian Church (1:8).

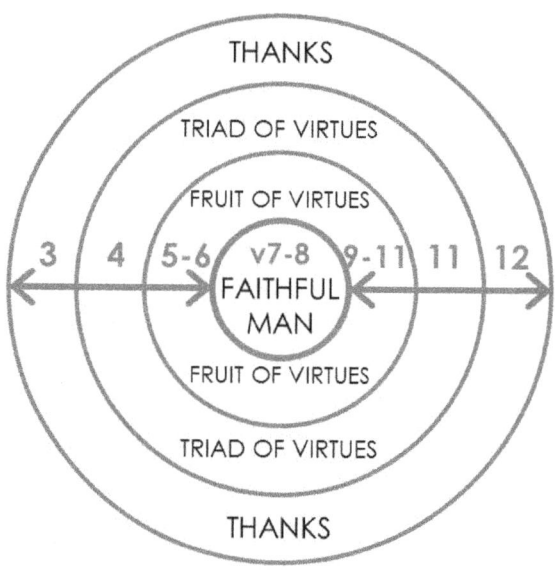

Fig. C – Colossians 1:3-12 chiasmus

On this basis, in the first strophe, Paul gives thanks for the Colossian Christians' *faith* and *love* (1:4), which has flowed from their *hope* (1:5). This triad of virtues, which

Martin calls "a handy compendium of early church qualities" (cf. Rom 5:1-5; 1 Cor 13:13; Gal 5:5-6; Eph 1:15, 18; 4:2-5; 1 Thes 1:3; 5:8; Heb 6:10-12; 10:22-24; 1 Pet 1:3-8, 21, 22),[55] and which Lucas notes are the consequence, not the cause, of God's work in their life,[56] is the evidence that Paul cites to prove their participation in Christ.[57] By trusting in the power and grace of God displayed in Jesus (faith),[58] they prove that they live under his lordship and have been incorporated into him.[59] By living lives of self-sacrifice[60] and concern for all God's people (love),[61] "true humanity reaches its highest potential."[62] By pursuing the promises of the future harvest (hope), they receive and exercise the first-fruits in the present.[63]

This is then reinforced when we examine the second strophe (1:9-11), which also displays a chiastic pattern that has tended to be overlooked by interpreters. Verses 9 and

---

[55] Martin, *Colossians and Philemon*, 47; cf. O'Brien, *Colossians, Philemon*, 11.
[56] Lucas, *The Message of Colossians and Philemon*, 27.
[57] Keck particularly links the significance of anticipation (i.e., hope) and participation as the key hallmarks of salvation, living in the present according to the age to come: Keck, *Paul And His Letters*, 75-78; Cf. Wright, *Colossians and Philemon*, 55.
[58] Dunn, *Colossians and Philemon*, 56.
[59] O'Brien, *Colossians, Philemon*, 11.
[60] Dunn, *Colossians and Philemon*, 58.
[61] Wright, *Colossians and Philemon*, 55.
[62] Barclay, *Colossians and Philemon*, 89.
[63] Thompson, *Colossians and Philemon*, 20.

11 each aspire to their own triads: first, the blessings of "knowledge of God's will," "wisdom," and "understanding" (1:9); second, the virtues of "strength/endurance," "patience," and "joy" (1:11). Thus the effect of this second triad of virtues is not only to mirror the first triad of faith, love, and hope within the wider chiastic scheme, but also to stand aside the second strophe's triad of blessings to point inwards to what they underpin: "lives worthy of the Lord, fully pleasing to him" (1:10).

As noted above, there are indications that Paul uses these signs of the Spirit's work among them to offer a vision for where they are heading, rather than congratulating them for having already arrived. In response to these virtues, Paul feels the need to petition God for the "spiritual wisdom and understanding" that should follow (1:9), which may imply a distinction between the wisdom and understanding they have and that which they need.

This naturally draws our eye to the later warning against "philosophy" that is "according to human tradition, according to the elemental spirits of the universe, and not according to Christ" (2:8). Thus it may be that while Paul is encouraged by the first-fruits of their faith, he is concerned for them to grow into greater maturity in Christ if they are to truly live as they have been called.

It is therefore significant that what he prays for are the hallmarks of relationship, authority, and agency displayed in the examples of true humanity he has called attention to. He calls for a relationship with God that empowers their faith with sensitivity to His guidance, and resonance with His moral heart (1:9). He calls for authority that fulfils their hope with the strength and power of the kingdom (1:11).[64] Finally, he calls for their lives to be energised with love that flows from the fruits of the Spirit (1:11 cf. Gal 5:22).[65] What Paul envisions, then, as the heart of each strophe indicates, is the full process of Christian transformation, from responding to the gospel to living in the fullness of God's pleasure.

In each case this is described as "bearing fruit" (vv.6, 10), a phrase that resonates with echoes from the Genesis vision of humanity made in the image of God (Gen 1:26-28). As Christopher Beetham notes, comparing with the LXX, this "displays a remarkable similarity in wording, thought, and cadence to the celebrated phrase found in Gen 1:28."[66] In which case, Paul connects these blessings directly to the original call of humanity. By walking in faith, love, and hope, the church becomes fundamentally more human.

---

[64] Thompson, *Colossians and Philemon*, 26.
[65] O'Brien, *Colossians, Philemon*, 24.
[66] Beetham, *Echoes of Scripture*, 52; cf. Wright, *Colossians and Philemon*, 57-58; Barth and Blanke, *Colossians*, 158; Martin, *Colossians and Philemon*, 49; O'Brien, *Colossians, Philemon*, 13.

Chapter Three

EXEMPLIFIED IN CHRIST

Colossians 1:13-23

The switch in narrative voice from second person ("May you ...," Col 1:12) to first person in Colossians 1:13 ("He has rescued us ...") indicates that Paul's focus has shifted away from thanksgiving towards the themes he raised within it, beginning with an elaborate confession extending through 1:13-20, which celebrates in sequence the saving work of God, the supremacy of Christ, and the consequent reconciliation of humanity. The liturgical flavour of this section is well established, and it has been speculated that v.13-14 represents a baptismal creed,[67] or confession,[68] while v.15-20 is drawn from a hymn of the early church,[69]

---

[67] E.g., Barclay, *Colossians and Philemon*, 59; cf. Wall, *Colossians and Philemon*, 55-57; Lincoln, *Colossians*, 596.
[68] O'Brien, *Colossians, Philemon*, 32.
[69] E.g., O'Brien, *Colossians, Philemon*, 32; Barth and Blanke, *Colossians*, 194; Dunn, *Colossians and Philemon*, 83.

and v.21-23 is Paul's exposition of the hymn.[70] On the one hand, this offers a microcosm of a worship service, into which Paul inserts himself (unfamiliar to them personally, Col 1:4, 8, 9; 2:1, 5) as a visiting teacher working within the community's own liturgical life. On the other, it effectively uses familiar words to reveal something radically new: the reality of a renewed identity in Christ.

The division I am proposing here is not without controversy. Typically, interpreters want to draw a clear distinction between vv.13-14 and vv.15-20,[71] with some preferring to connect vv.13-14 with the preceding thanksgiving.[72] Clearly there is a connection between these units, given the obvious link between the inheritance of light (1:12) and the power of darkness (1:13), but that may be explained by the careful unifying influence of the author. A more pertinent problem may be the apparent incongruence with the so-called "Christ hymn" (Col 1:15-20) that follows, which appears to stand alone as a distinct

---

[70] Cf. Dunn, *Colossians and Philemon*, 105; Wall, *Colossians and Philemon*, 77-78.
[71] Cf. Martin, *Colossians and Philemon*, 53-57; Lincoln, *Colossians*, 595-97.
[72] O'Brien, *Colossians, Philemon*, 25; Lucas, *The Message of Colossians and Philemon*, 35-43; Moo speculates that vv.13-14 may stand as an extended inclusio, closing the thanksgiving starting at v.3: Moo, *Colossians and Philemon*, 81-82.

unit, whether as a hymn, creed or liturgy,[73] indicated in part by the sudden loss of either first or second person referents, which only return at v.21. However, this distinction may be overstated. Indeed, it is important to note that while the identification of v.15-20 as an external text that has been included or, more likely, reworked by Paul for his own purposes, is proposed by many,[74] there remains scepticism on this point, with others claiming it as a solely Pauline composition.[75] In fact, I am inclined to think that Paul *has* drawn his words from the liturgical life of the Colossian church, but the lack of any scholarly consensus on this point serves to question the presence of a significant shift in tone at verse 15.

Whereas there are important reasons to see a transition at verse 13 and continuity between verses 14 and 15. In addition to the shift in perspective from second to first person at verse 13, there is also a shift in emphasis from subject (the church) to object (God, and then Jesus), and

---

[73] A view on which of these is in play will become pertinent when we revisit Paul's use of image of God language in Part Two, and will be discussed there.

[74] E.g. Thompson, *Colossians and Philemon*, 27-28; Dunn, *Colossians and Philemon*, 83-84; Arnold, *The Colossian Syncretism*, 6.

[75] For a measured example of this view, see Wright's counter-claim that it is not an insertion but is Paul's own poetic inflection: Wright, *Colossians and Philemon*, 68-70; N. T. Wright, *The Climax of the Covenant: Christ and the Law in Pauline Theology* (Minneapolis: T & T Clark, 1993), 99-106.

while the referents disappear at verse 15, the emphasis on Christ continues into the hymn. We should also note that, having opened the unit by shifting the object from God to Christ in v.13 ("the kingdom of his [God's] beloved *Son*" – emphasis mine), Paul closes it by shifting the object back from Christ to God in v.20 ("through him [Jesus] *God* was pleased ..." – emphasis mine).

N. T. Wright has also argued that the use of ὅς ἐστιν (hos estin, "who is") at verse 15 suggests that it is intended to flow from the statement before.[76] After all, had Paul not spoken of the "beloved Son" in v.13, there would be considerable ambiguity as to the identity of the "who" in v.15. This is an important observation whether "who is" is a part of the original hymn, which Paul has cleverly weaved in at this point, or if he has added it himself. Either way, he intends it to be read *in this context*, in connection to vv.13-14. In which case, this section would open with a single sentence, offering a biography of Jesus:

> He [God] has rescued us from the power of darkness and transferred us into the kingdom of his beloved Son, in whom we have redemption, the forgiveness of sins, who is the image of the invisible God, the firstborn of all creation.
>
> Colossians 1:13-15

---

[76] Wright, *Colossians and Philemon*, 68.

More pointedly, following the chiasmus in the preceding verses, a second chiastic unit can be identified in vv.13-20. Markus Barth and Helmut Blanke, in their commentary, and N. T. Wright in his, both identify the use of parallelism in v.15-20,[77] but if we read back to include v.13-14, we find a pattern more sophisticated than Barth and Blanke's and less complicated than Wright's (see Fig. D).

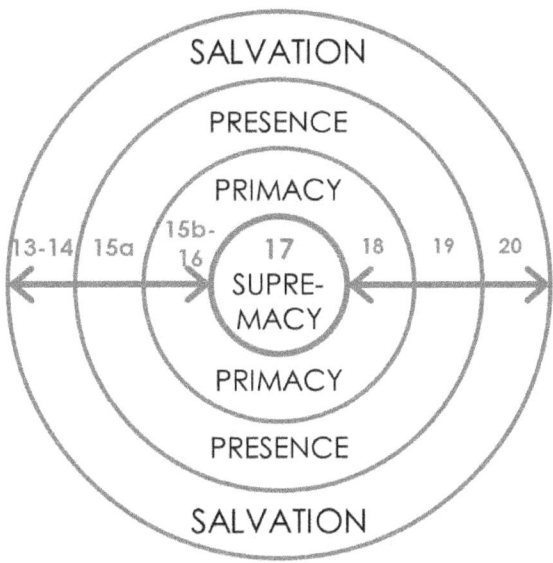

Fig. D – Colossians 1:13-20 chiasmus

---

[77] Barth and Blanke, *Colossians*, 194; Wright, *Colossians and Philemon*, 69-70.

The Colossian Image

In this scheme, the saving work of the cross, referred to at 1:13-14 and 1:20, becomes the way in to see the true nature of Christ, who bears the presence of God,[78] is the firstborn in both creation and the Church, and is therefore supreme over all things. Seen in this light, I believe the unity of vv.13-20 becomes clear, even if that unity is the result of Paul's careful weaving together of separate sources.

This is not to challenge the identification of vv.15-20 as a distinct unit, which has in my view been well established,[79] but it may contribute to the discussion about how Paul worked with the Colossian liturgy to edit it together for his own ends.[80] Not that vv.13-14 stands as an introduction to the "Christ hymn," as Christopher Stanley infers,[81] but that together they tell a story of their own, which when combined with Paul's subsequent

---

[78] My argument that Paul's use of "image" (εἰκών, eikon) here is a reference not only to Genesis 1, but to the indwelling presence of God that the Hebrew צֶלֶם (tselem, "image") implies, will be unpacked in detail in chapters 6 and 9.

[79] For a particularly developed defence of this, see Wright, *Colossians and Philemon*, 68-74. Dunn offers his own defence, but also acknowledges aspects in the second half (Col 1:18b-20) that scan less poetically than the first half, which may cast doubt on whether it is a single unit, and concedes it can never be known for sure if it is an insertion at all. Nevertheless, this is the view he maintains: Dunn, *Colossians and Philemon*, 83-87.

[80] As exemplified in the discussions referenced on page 63.

[81] Stanley, *Paul and Scripture*, 193.

Exemplified in Christ

commentary (vv.21-23) serve to lift the church out of its estrangement (cf. 1:21) and locate them within the wider narrative of God's saving action towards His people.

We have already seen how Paul's greeting alludes to the position of the Colossian church within the people of God. To a church very likely made up of both Gentiles and Jews[82] this not only asserts the unity of the diverse brethren, but it makes the radical claim that the Gentiles are now to be considered a part of the people of Israel. Paul then develops this claim as he turns from thanksgiving to begin his Christological exegesis.

The bridge between the two comes as Paul exalts "the Father who has enabled you to share in the inheritance of the saints in the light" (1:12b), in response to a life of faith, love, and hope. This reference to inheritance evokes the covenantal promise made to Israel, who share in the inheritance of the land and, indeed, the inheritance of God himself (Num 33:54; Deut 4:20; 10:9).[83] Whether this alludes to a specific passage, or is only an echo of a significant theme,[84] Paul's intent is clear: to cement the assertion of his greeting, that the Colossian church are

---

[82] As per Wright, *Colossians and Philemon*, 24-25.
[83] Beetham, *Echoes of Scripture*, 81-82.
[84] For a discussion on the differences and respective impacts of allusions and echoes, see Hays, *Echoes of Scripture*, 18-21; Beetham, *Echoes of Scripture*, 15-24; Stanley, *Paul and Scripture*, 185-86.

indeed among the saints of God, in covenant with the Father, who share in Christ's heavenly inheritance.

What then follows in vv.13-20 is a masterful compilation of Colossian liturgy which is packed with echoes of and allusions to the Old Testament narrative, as Paul invites the Colossian Christians to see their place within the story of Israel, set within the wider frame of the story of all creation. It has been commonly observed that vv.13-14 evokes the Exodus story, referring both to rescue (Col 1:13 cf. Ex 3:8) and redemption (Col 1:14 cf. Ex 6:6).[85] However, in light of Jeremiah 23:7-8, which calls for a shift towards Israel's rescue from Babylon as the pinnacle moment of God's saving activity, displacing the exodus (cf. Isa 31:4-5; Mic 4:10), we must at least allow for the exile in Paul's thoughts here.[86]

Indeed, it is likely that he intends both to resonate, as he places before the Colossians the centrepiece events in Israel's faith story. Concurrently, there is also an echo of God's promise of an everlasting kingdom to David (Col 1:13 cf. 2 Sam 7:5-16). Thus Paul summarises with exquisite efficiency the enduring narrative of the Jewish nation, who had incorporated God's former acts of salvation and

---

[85] E.g., Walsh and Keesmaat, *Colossians Remixed*, 109; Stanley, *Paul and Scripture*, 193-96; Beetham, *Echoes of Scripture*, 91-95.
[86] This appears to be in Peter's mind as he equates the dispersion of the early church with exile: 1 Peter 1:1, 17; 2:11. There may also be a hint of this in Hebrews 11:13.

Exemplified in Christ

restoration into its religious life, indicating that once more God was intervening to save and restore His people.

Most appropriately, then, these lead into the most striking and fundamental allusion of all, to the Creation, which not only evokes the original human design to which the Colossians are being conformed, but provokes them to consider how this has been reimagined, enhanced even, by the death and resurrection of Christ. We have already noted the references to light and darkness (Col 1:12, 13 cf. Gen 1:2, 3), which stand as echoes before the explicit allusions to Genesis 1 that dominate the "Christ hymn." Here Paul's high Christology comes to the fore as he identifies Christ not only as the image of God (Col 1:15 cf. Gen 1:26-28; 9:6) - that is, the personification of true humanity - but also the Creator who is imaged (1:16 cf. Gen 1:1; Neh 9:6; Isa 44:24; 66:2).

I do not propose to unpack the full implications of these claims at this point, except to acknowledge their importance in the cosmology and ecclesiology that follows. Instead, I will return to this as the focus of a more detailed study in Part Two. For now, what matters is that we see how Paul applies these claims, for these are not casual associations but assertions of Christ's power to reconcile to God that which he rules.

He does this not by conquest, as in the Exodus (Ex 3:19-22), nor by subversion, as in the Exile (2 Chr 36:22-23), but by incarnation (Jn 1:14). By entering into the cosmos, Jesus claimed the authority of the firstborn of creation (Col 1:15-16); by entering in to humanity, he claimed the inheritance not only of Israel (God's firstborn son, Ex 4:22), but of Adam (the firstborn human, Gen 2:7), which he in turn extended to the ekklesia (Col 1:18).

Thus when he submitted to the cross, thereby defeating sin, corruption and death, his inheritance became one of salvation and reconciliation for all who bear the hallmarks of his family, and renewed commission for all who bear the hallmarks of his image (Col 1:20-23). In other words, Paul asserts that through its association with Christ the church enters into Israel's story, receiving the inheritance of its past rescue, its present redemption, and its future resurrection. At the same time, they are recreated as a new humanity as they are reconciled, with the rest of creation, through Christ.[87]

---

[87] Cf. Thompson, *Colossians and Philemon*, 40.

Chapter Four

LIVING A CRUCIFORM LIFE

Colossians 1:24-2:5

We have already seen that a key aspect of this letter is Paul's elevation of others - namely Christ, himself and Epaphras - as models for the Colossians to emulate in their Christian faith, and how this offers a window in to Paul's vision of true humanity. Having centred his thanksgiving on the example of Epaphras (Col 1:7-8), followed by a confession of Christ through whom all humanity may be restored (1:13-23),[88] Paul now presents his own walk of faith in greater detail (1:24-2:5).

This change in emphasis occurs in 1:23b with another shift in first person referents, this time regarding authorial voice, as Paul shifts from speaking of "us/our/we" (1:3, 4, 8, 9), referring to both himself and Timothy (1:1), to "I, Paul."[89] Consistent with a typically Pauline letter

---

[88] He returns to Christ as an exemplar in Colossians 3:1-17.
[89] Barclay, *Colossians and Philemon*, 20; Wall, *Colossians and Philemon*, 85.

structure, he uses this shift to discuss, as James Dunn puts it, "his own missionary labours and personal involvement with his readers" (cf. Rom 1:11-15; 15:14-32; 1 Cor 16:1-11; Gal 1:10-2:21; Phil 1:12-26; 1 Thes 2:17-3:11; Phm 21-22),[90] thereby clarifying his reasons for writing ("... so that *we* may present everyone mature in Christ. For this *I* toil ...," Col 1:28-29), and projecting his own life before the church both as a justification of his apostolic authority and an example to imitate.[91] In particular, the aspect of his faith that he stresses is his communion with Christ, which is evidenced by his outward actions (1:24-25, 29; 2:1), his inner wisdom (1:26-27), and the fruit of his labour (1:28; 2:2-5).

As Douglas Moo has noted, Colossians 1:24-2:5 can be isolated as a distinct unit by the presence of a third chiastic arrangement, which he identifies according to the use of mirrored vocabulary, in which the A/A' clauses (1:24; 2:5) refer to χαίρω (chairo, "rejoice") and σάρξ (sarx, "flesh"/"body"), the B/B' clauses (1:27; 2:2) emphasise γνωρίζω/ἐπίγνωσις (gnorizo, "make known"/epignosis, "knowledge"), πλοῦτος, (ploutos, "riches") and μυστήριον (mysterion, "mystery"), and the vertex (1:29; 2:1) describes Paul's ἀγωνιζομαι/ἀγών (agonizomai/agon, "struggle"):

---

[90] Dunn, *Colossians and Philemon*, 113; cf. Moo, *Colossians and Philemon*, 148.
[91] Cf. Wright, *Colossians and Philemon*, 90; Martin, *Colossians and Philemon*, 69; Wall, *Colossians and Philemon*, 83.

A: "I am now rejoicing [χαίρω] ... and in my flesh [σαρκί] ..." Col 1:24

   B – "To them God chose to make known [γνωρίσαι] ... the riches [πλοῦτος] of the glory of this mystery [μυστηρίου] ..." Col 1:27

      C – "For this I toil and struggle [ἀγωνιζόμενος] ..." Col 1:29

      C' – "I want you to know how much I am struggling [ἀγῶνα] ..." Col 2:1

   B' – "... they may have all the riches [πλοῦτος] ... and have the knowledge [ἐπίγνωσιν] of God's mystery [μυστηρίου] ..." Col 2:2

A' – "I am absent in body [σαρκὶ] ... I rejoice [χαίρων] to see your morale ..." Col 2:5[92]

This mirrored vocabulary confirms a coherent literary unit, which can be expanded into a fully developed chiasmus when we consider the thematic as well as the literary progression. However, I would differ in my delineation of the chiasmus from Moo in one respect, by drawing verse 28 into the vertex, which shifts the emphasis slightly, but importantly, from Paul's struggle to his motivation (see Fig. E).

---

[92] Moo, *Colossians and Philemon*, 148.

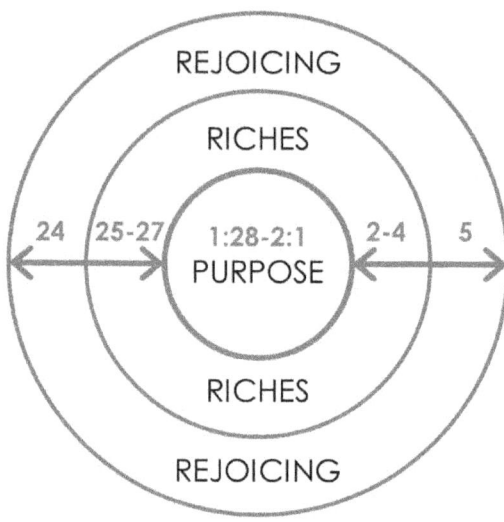

Fig. E – Colossians 1:24-2:5 chiasmus

In this scheme the outer clauses highlight Paul's joyful *response* to his calling and the Colossians' growth. This then leads to the *source* of Paul's authority and energy; that is, the mystery of God's indwelling presence (1:27). Finally, the vertex indicates the *motivation* that drives him, and sustains him in his efforts: to participate in Christ, and to see others attain the same maturity. Peter O'Brien notes a different "circular" division by Franz Zeilinger, who argued for a more compact unit (vv.1:24-29), in which the vertex is the mystery of Christ (1:26-27), surrounded by comments on the apostle's task (1:25, 28) and the apostle's suffering/struggle (1:24, 29).[93] O'Brien is sceptical, but interestingly it is supported by a similar but shorter arrangement to Col 2:1-5, in which the vertex is once again the mystery of Christ (Col 2:2-3), surrounded by references to Paul's connection to them from a distance (Col 2:1, 4-5). This compliments the message of the overarching chiasmus I am proposing here, and corresponds to the indication of two chiasms forming one larger chiastic unit that I identified in Paul's earlier thanksgiving (Col 1:3-12). As such, it may be a valuable area for further study.

It is often speculated that the enigmatic language used in this section is designed to appeal to a church that is drawn to the allure of possessing secret knowledge, whether that is rooted in a Jewish, gnostic, or otherwise pagan heresy.[94] This is something we will discuss in more detail in chapter twelve. For now, what matters is the function of this language, which draws the Colossian Christians to want what he has, and to understand both the reward and the cost this entails. The reward, expressed as the knowledge of God's mystery (Col 1:26, 27; 2:2), is directly connected to the prior confession of Christ. Just as God is in Christ

---

[93] O'Brien, *Colossians, Philemon*, 74.
[94] Arnold, *The Colossian Syncretism*, 271-72; Lucas, *The Message of Colossians and Philemon*, 69; Thompson, *Colossians and Philemon*, 42; Martin, *Colossians and Philemon*, 73; cf. Wall, *Colossians and Philemon*, 91.

(1:19), Christ is in us (1:27). Thus there is a direct communion with God the Father through Jesus the Son, characterised by this concentric relationship of indwelling presence. Indeed, it may be that Paul utilises a chiastic/concentric structure for so much of this letter because it subversively conveys the message that Christian identity is rooted in a series of concentric relationships: God within Christ (1:19; 2:9), Christ within Christians (1:27), God within Christians (2:10), especially by His Spirit (1:8), and Christians living in Christ (2:6-11).

The cost is expressed in terms of suffering. The claim that draws the eye in this section is Paul's startling statement that "in my flesh I am completing what is lacking in Christ's afflictions for the sake of his body, the church" (1:24). This claim has long caused confusion and consternation to scholars and lay Christians alike. The troubling implication on first read, as Andrew Lincoln notes, is that Paul considers the cross to have been somehow insufficient for salvation. However, this seems highly at odds with the tone of the preceding exaltation of the Christ hymn, which declares that "through him [Christ] God was pleased to reconcile to himself *all things*, whether on earth or in heaven, by making peace through the blood of his cross" (1:20, emphasis mine).[95]

---

[95] Lincoln, *Colossians*, 613.

We might be tempted to explain this by pointing to Paul's incorporation of external material, to draw a distinction between the exaltation of the liturgy he inserts and his own beliefs, but this only solves one problem by creating two others. First, that Paul is content to commend texts he does not fully endorse; and second, that Paul's theology of the cross is that it is an incomplete Gospel. However, in light of his categorical words in 1 Corinthians that "we proclaim Christ crucified ... For I decided to know nothing among you except Jesus Christ, and him crucified" (1 Cor 2:2), this seems unlikely and we must find a better explanation for Paul's claim.

Many point to a Jewish apocalyptic eschatology underpinning Paul's claim here, in which he anticipates that the transfer from the "present evil age" (Gal 1:4) into the "age to come" (Eph 1:21)[96] will be initiated by what some Jewish apocalyptic writing described as "the woes of the Messiah."[97] Briefly, this foresaw that the final victory of the Messiah would be preceded by a time of affliction, just as slavery and exile had preceded God's salvation from Egypt and Babylon respectively, and that the participation of God's people in this affliction was an essential step towards the fulfilment of God's timing and

---

[96] Cf. Colossians 1:27: "the hope of glory."
[97] E.g. O'Brien, *Colossians, Philemon*, 78-79; Lohse, *Colossians and Philemon*, 70-72; Martin, *Colossians and Philemon*, 70; Wright, *Colossians and Philemon*, 91-92.

a key signpost of impending salvation. An example of this eschatology can be found in the Jewish text 1 Enoch:

> In that day the holy ones who live above the heavens will assemble and, with united voice, petition, supplicate, praise, laud, and bless the name of the Lord of hosts, on account of the blood of the righteous which has been shed ... At once I beheld the Ancient of Days sitting upon the throne of his glory, and the book of life was opened in his presence ... Then the hearts of the saints were full of joy, because the consummation of righteousness had arrived, the prayers of the saints heard, and the blood of the righteous appreciated by the Lord of hosts.
>
> 1 Enoch 47:2-4

James Dunn furthers this thought by discussing the correlation between Colossians 1:24 and other texts such as 4 Ezra 4:33-43, which refers to a time "when the number of those like yourselves is completed" (v.36). In which case, what is in view is "an appointed sum of suffering that must be endured in order to trigger (as it were) the final events of history."[98]

---

[98] Dunn, *Colossians and Philemon*, 114-16.

On the other hand, N. T. Wright has observed that nowhere does the New Testament actually use θλῖψις (thlipsis, "affliction") in reference to the cross.[99] In which case, whatever Paul claims to be incomplete, it is not the saving work of the cross. Instead, Wright argues, Paul is "putting into practice the principle of which Calvary was, in one sense, the supreme outworking."[100] Similarly, Markus Barth and Helmut Blanke have argued that for Paul, suffering is the pinnacle of Christ-likeness, and Colossians 1:24 is therefore "an essential and substantial component of the concept of Pauline service."[101] In other words, Paul has chosen to adopt (and therefore commends) a sacrificial life, in which suffering is a practical reality, so that he might attain the Christlikeness that is not yet complete *in himself.*

What is lacking, then, is not Christ's suffering, but the completion of Paul's Christ-like calling *on behalf of* the Church.[102] Indeed, Paul goes on to clarify that he is only

---

[99] Wright, *Colossians and Philemon*, 93; cf. Thompson, *Colossians and Philemon*, 44-45.
[100] Wright, *Colossians and Philemon*, 93.
[101] Barth and Blanke, *Colossians*, 295.
[102] Cf. Moo, *Colossians and Philemon*, 150-51. Lincoln argues for a more cautionary interpretation, highlighting a variation in the understanding of messianic woes in other first and second century texts (e.g., 2 Bar 20; 25; 4 Ez 4:12, 33-37; 13:16-19), which suggests Colossians was written at a time prior to this theological idea taking root: Lincoln, *Colossians*, 614. Nevertheless, the use of θλῖψις (thlipsis) to describe the

able to bear the "toil and struggle" because of "the energy that he [Christ] powerfully inspires within me" (Col 1:29), so that he places his own sufferings under the umbrella of Christ's strength, demonstrated most powerfully on the cross. Thus, Paul is sharing in Christ's sufferings, not adding to them.[103] The privilege and promise of this level of participation in Christ's suffering is a repeated catalyst for Paul's joy (Col 1:24; cf. Rom 5:3; 8:18; 2 Cor 1:5-7; 4:17-18; 7:4; 1 Thes 1:6), since it opens the way both to communion with Christ and salvation in Christ.[104]

In the same vein, Peter O'Brien has highlighted the importance of θλῖψις (thlipsis, "affliction") as the word used in the LXX to describe the suffering of Israel in the narrative accounts of exodus and exile (Ex 4:31; Deut 4:29; 28:47-68; Jdg 6:9; 10:6-16; 1 Sam 10:18-19; 2 Kgs 19:3).[105] This accentuates the emphasis Paul places on participation with Christ, whereby his suffering is not in addition to Christ's suffering, but *is* Christ's suffering, in the sense that because he is a member of the body of Christ, he

---

apocalyptic transition of ages, consistent with the LXX's similar use to describe the transitions in the pre-post-exodus-exile ages discussed above, and in conjunction with other apocalyptic language such as μυστήριον (mysterion, "mystery," Dan 2:18-19, 27-30; 4 Ez 14:5; 1 En 51:3; 103:2), is not to be dismissed.
[103] Dunn, *Colossians and Philemon*, 114.
[104] Dunn, *Colossians and Philemon*, 114.
[105] O'Brien, *Colossians, Philemon*, 79.

endures the suffering that goes hand in hand with participating in the mission of Christ.[106]

Michael Gorman calls this cruciformity, which he defines as "*participating in* and *embodying* the cross," which looks like "conformity to the image of God's son"[107] (Rom 8:29; 2 Cor 3:18; cf. Phil 3:10 and especially Col 3:10), which is "not merely a conformity to his suffering – though it includes that (e.g., Rom 8:17; Phil 3:10) – but conformity to his cross-shaped narrative."[108] In light of the assurance of resurrection with Christ (Col 1:18) and reconciliation to God (Col 1:20-23) already discussed, what Paul offers here is a covenantal exchange whereby as the Church participates in its cruciform life, it is transformed into the renewed humanity in Christ.

As such, it is this vision of cruciformity, expressed in his own life, which Paul hopes to pass on to the Colossian Christians. He assures them that his suffering is for their sake (Col 1:24), and he expresses his desire for them to emulate the same self-sacrificial love (Col 2:2) so that they might experience the same richness of wisdom and knowledge in Christ (Col 2:3) that they recognise in his life. That is, that they would also share in Christ's

---

[106] Thompson, *Colossians and Philemon*, 45; Dunn, *Colossians and Philemon*, 116.
[107] Gorman, *Reading Paul*, 146.
[108] Gorman, *Reading Paul*, 147.

sufferings in order to attain to Christ's indwelling presence.

In pursuit of this hope, Paul affirms his commitment to "warning everyone and teaching everyone in all wisdom, so that we may present everyone mature [τέλειον, teleion] in Christ" (Col 1:28b cf. 1:22). Here again, Paul's pursuit of maturity suggests a high anthropology at work, carrying implications of completeness or even 'perfection'. Gorman presses this even further to assert a process of theosis,[109] such that humanity is elevated to its perfect state as it attains the likeness of Christ, "who is the *telos* of human existence."[110]

---

[109] Gorman, *Inhabiting the Cruciform God*, 90-93.
[110] Gorman, *Inhabiting the Cruciform God*, 162.

Chapter Five

SHARING IN THE RESURRECTION

Colossians 2:6-3:4

It is well attested that Colossians 2:6 marks the break between an extended introduction and the main body of the letter.[111] Up to this point, Paul's Christological emphasis has centred on a premise: Jesus is Lord. In the material that follows (2:6-4:6), Paul's emphasis shifts to the impact of this premise ("continue to live your lives in him," Col 2:6).[112] Thus he develops the theme of attaining to Christlikeness that he introduced in the previous section, as he turns his attention to where (or rather, in whom) the Colossians' lives should be rooted (Col 2:6-19), and how this should be lived out (Col 2:20-3:4; 3:5-4:6).[113]

---

[111] E.g., see Dunn, *Colossians and Philemon*, 136; O'Brien, *Colossians, Philemon*, 104-05.
[112] Moo, *Colossians and Philemon*, 175.
[113] Dunn, *Colossians and Philemon*, 136; Moo, *Colossians and Philemon*, 177.

The Colossian Image

He begins by revisiting his first affirmation for the Colossians: that they are "in Christ" (Col 1:2). This unfolds in another chiastic unit (Col 2:6-19) which explicates what this means through eight positive statements regarding life "in him" or "with him" (Col 2:6, 7, 9, 10, 11, 12 [twice], 13). He then follows this with a vision for what this life looks like in practice (Col 3:1-4; 3:12-4:1).

Running alongside these positive assertions, however, are cautionary warnings against spiritually unhealthy influences and practices that will detract from the Colossians' faith (Col 2:8, 16-23; 3:5-9),[114] and it is these — particularly the nature of the dangerous influence(s) — that have tended to dominate the discussion surrounding Paul's portrayal of life "in Christ." I will reserve a detailed analysis of both of Paul's warning and his commission to life "in Christ" for Part Three, when we will reflect on how Paul's anthropology, as we have unpacked it in Part One, works in relation to his understanding of the image of God, which we will examine in Part Two. Nevertheless, there are a few important observations that will suffice to outline here as we collate our findings thus far and prepare to turn our attention to an analysis of Paul's use of "image of God" language.

Firstly, God's plan for humanity is to live *according to Christ* (Col 2:8). Paul makes this point amid the dangers

---

[114] Cf. Moo, *Colossians and Philemon*, 183.

Sharing in the Resurrection

of living "according to human tradition" and "according to elemental spirits." We will return to a discussion about the disputed meaning of each of these statements in chapter twelve, but in doing so we can lose sight of Paul's primary intent; that is, to evoke in the Colossian Christians a dependence on Christ alone.[115] Recalling Colossians 1:19, he affirms that "in him the whole fullness of deity dwells bodily, and you have come to fullness in him" (Col 2:9-10 cf. 1:19).

It has been claimed that Paul uses πλήρωμα (pleroma, "fullness") in different senses for Christ and humanity here. Peter O'Brien, for example, argues that any suggestion of a fullness of deity in Colossians 2:10 is unlikely, since Paul's references to 'fullness' elsewhere concern qualities of godliness. As such, he prefers to read "and you have come to fullness *of life* in him."[116]

However, given their close proximity, the use of καὶ (kai, "and") to connect them, and the framing of both within a single "in him" statement, which Paul uses consistently to describe the relevance of Christ to the Colossians, it is far more likely that the same sense of "fullness" is intended. Only by living according to Christ can humanity attain fullness, both in the sense of maturity, as described in

---

[115] Moo, *Colossians and Philemon*, 193; cf. Thompson, *Colossians and Philemon*, 54.
[116] O'Brien, *Colossians, Philemon*, 113. Lincoln argues similarly: Lincoln, *Colossians*, 623.

The Colossian Image

Colossians 1:28 – i.e. becoming complete – and bearing the presence of God, as in Col 1:19.[117]

However, while the same meaning applies for Christ and for the Colossians, the implications of that meaning differ. For Christ, it means the revelation of his divinity in glory. As John Barclay has said of Colossians 2:9, "That gets about as near to calling Christ 'God' as it is possible to go without actually doing so."[118] For the Colossians, it means the attainment of true humanity, operating out of the authority and power of God as He dwells within them, which is accessed only in Christ. He is the fulcrum that moves the presence, the power, and the authority of God from heaven to earth.[119]

Secondly, God's plan for humanity is to live *according to the resurrection*. This comes to the fore when we note the chiasmus at play in Colossians 2:6-19 (see Fig. F). Here we find that Paul's warnings are pushed to the edge, whereas participation in Christ's death and resurrection is drawn into the vertex (Col 2:12). We will analyse this in detail in chapter twelve, but what is immediately clear is that the Colossians' life "in Christ" is principally a life of resurrection.

---

[117] Cf. Gorman, *Inhabiting the Cruciform God*, 4-5; see also Blackwell, "You Are Filled In Him" *Journal of Theological Interpretation* .
[118] Barclay, *Colossians and Philemon*, 81.
[119] Cf. Arnold, *The Colossian Syncretism*, 294-95.

Sharing in the Resurrection

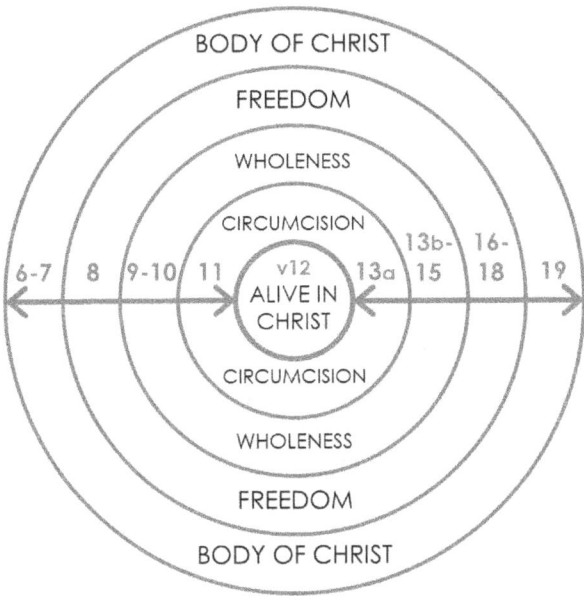

Fig. F – Colossians 2:6-19 chiasmus

Paul associates this resurrection life with the rite of baptism (2:12), in which a profound identity shift occurs as the baptismal waters take on the role of Christ's tomb, which we escape with Jesus as a new person, receiving God's life-giving power in Christ, as he exercises his sovereign authority to forgive (Col 2:13), and sharing in Christ's triumph over "rulers and authorities" (Col 2:10, 15). The emphasis is once more on participation, and the effect is to assure the church that while they continue to experience the realities of the present evil age, they are already complete,[120] and have in a very real sense been raised "to share in the resurrection life of the new epoch."[121]

Participating in Christ

In the segue that follows in Colossians 2:20-3:4,[122] this is reinforced as Paul discusses the cosmic implications of their resurrection. Deviating for the first time from chiasm, he offers a simple two-strophe parallelism, delineated by the conditional εἰ (ei, "if"), to open each strophe (see Fig. G) to argue that the natural response to a life that has been recreated through Christ's death and resurrection is to live as participants of the heavenly realm even as they remain in the earthly realm. Therefore, Paul urges them to "seek the things that are above" (Col 3:1), living the heavenly lives they are now empowered to live.[123]

---

[120] Cf. Wright, *Colossians and Philemon*, 101, 113; Wall, *Colossians and Philemon*, 115.

[121] Dunn, *Colossians and Philemon*, 161; cf. Wright, *Colossians and Philemon*, 101; O'Brien, *Colossians, Philemon*, 120.

[122] Marianne Meye Thompson similarly argues for these verses forming a separate interim unit: Thompson, *Colossians and Philemon*, 69.

[123] Cf. Wright, *Colossians and Philemon*, 133-34; Thompson, *Colossians and Philemon*, 68-69; O'Brien, *Colossians, Philemon*, 159-60.

Sharing in the Resurrection

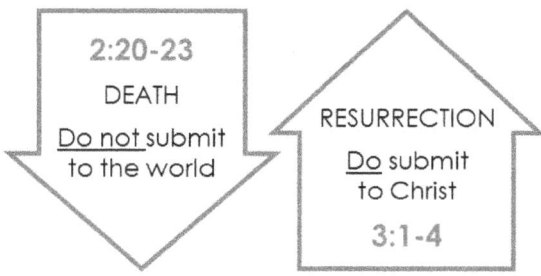

Fig. G – Colossians 2:20-3:4 parallelism

Finally, having been raised with Christ, Paul completes the circle as he affirms the Colossian Christians' *renewed identity as the image of God* (Col 3:10). Once more, this is emphasised by a chiasmus present in Col 3:5-17 (see Fig. H).[124] Here again, we will examine the implications that lie behind this image identity in Part Two, and scrutinise the life Paul envisages flowing from it in Part Three. For now, it serves to observe the effect of parallelism that has been carried from the preceding segue into this chiastic unit, which sets the hallmarks of the life we have stripped off by sharing Christ's death against the hallmarks of the new humanity we have put on by sharing in Christ's

---

[124] James Dunn delineates Colossians 3:5-17 as a single coherent unit, but does not see a chiastic structure: Dunn, *Colossians and Philemon*, 210-12. Peter O'Brien notes certain chiastic sentences within this unit, but does not recognise a chiastic structure to the whole: O'Brien, *Colossians, Philemon*, 174-75.

resurrection (Col 3:9b-10).[125] Reading through the list of virtues, one is struck by their specified connection to Christ (Col 3:13, 15, 16, 17) which indicates a new humanity that adopts his character as it participates in his resurrection.[126]

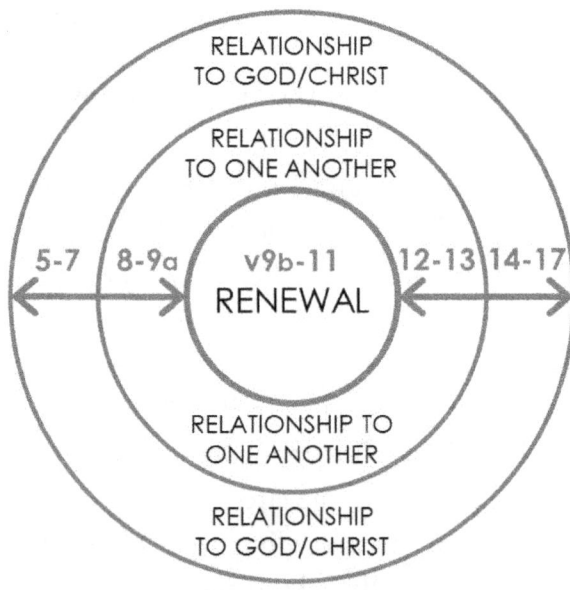

Fig. H – Colossians 3:5-17 chiasmus

---

[125] Moo, *Colossians and Philemon*, 252-55.
[126] Lucas, *The Message of Colossians and Philemon*, 150-51; Moo, *Colossians and Philemon*, 274.

Sharing in the Resurrection

Among these traits of new humanity, we find forgiveness (Col 3:13 cf. 1:14) and peace (Col 3:15 cf. 1:20), two marks of Christ's defeat over "the power of darkness" (Col 1:13). These are attained by putting on love, which "binds everything together" (Col 3:14 cf. 1:17) and letting "the word [λόγος, logos] of Christ dwell in you richly" (Col 3:16), which resonates with a potential Wisdom/Logos theology in play as Paul identifies Christ as "the image of the invisible God" (Col 1:15).[127] Thus, the vision of true humanity is one that shares the authority of Christ as it participates with him.[128]

It is at this point that Paul's Christological, anthropological and cosmological threads, which have run throughout the letter, converge to knit his message together. As the Colossian Christians participate in the death and resurrection of Christ through baptism, and as they pursue lives of cruciform Christlikeness, they are transformed into a renewed humanity. This new humanity finds its ultimate expression in the heavenly

---

[127] We will discuss this in chapter eight.
[128] Lincoln argues that as the church receives fullness through Christ, they effectively share in his authority to rule over the powers of the universe: Lincoln, *Colossians*, 623; cf. Moo, who sees it rather as the church living under the protection of their Lord, who exercises authority over their spiritual enemies: Moo, *Colossians and Philemon*, 196.

realms (Col 3:4), yet bears the same blessings as Christ in this world as it waits expectantly for glory.[129]

These blessings of fullness (Col 2:10), indicating the indwelling presence of God (cf. Col 1:19; 3:16), resurrection (Col 2:12-13), indicating the life-giving power of God (cf. Col 1:18; 3:1), authority (Col 2:10, 15 cf. Col 1:16; 3:14-15), and unity (Col 3:11), rooted in Christ's love, which holds all things together (cf. Col 1:17; 3:14), are the hallmarks of Paul's vision for true humanity, and are the basis on which he can claim that the Colossians have been renewed into the image of God (Col 3:10).

This, then, is the heart of Paul's underlying anthropology. Just as Christ is the image of God (Col 1:15), so too is the church, as the embodiment of true humanity, the image of its creator (3:10). And it is to a fuller understanding of what Paul means by this that we now turn in Part Two.

---

[129] Cf. Garland, *Colossians and Philemon*, 207; Wall, *Colossians and Philemon*, 143.

PART TWO
The Image of God in Colossians

> He is the image of the invisible God,
> the firstborn of all creation.
>
> Colossians 1:15

Chapter Six

CHRIST, THE IMAGE

If the underlying anthropological vision of Colossians is that New Covenant fidelity to Christ, expressed in a life of faith, love, and hope, results in a renewal of humanity as the image of God (Col 3:10), then it is essential that we consider carefully Paul's meaning when he refers to "image" (εἰκών, eikon). Such a study must begin by recognising that εἰκών is a word that would have resonated strongly with the first-century Church, rich as it is in cultural and religious significance.[130] On the one hand, living in the context of empire, where coins,[131] statues and monuments carrying the εἰκών of Caesar filled the Roman world, proclaiming his lordship, both earthly and divine,[132] any reference to Christ as a divinely appointed

---

[130] Moo, *Colossians and Philemon*, 111.
[131] Consider, for example, the only usage of εἰκών in the Gospels, referring to the image of Caesar on a coin (Mt 22:20, Mk 12:16, Lk 20:24).
[132] Gorman, *Apostle of the Crucified Lord*, 17; Horsley, *Paul and Empire*, 74.

The Colossian Image

εἰκών could imply a direct challenge to that lordship.[133] On the other hand, the church's inheritance of and entrance into the faith story of Israel would surely impress an allusion to humanity's creation as "the image of God" (εἰκόνα θεοῦ, eikona theou, Gen 1:27, LXX).[134] Moreover, the surrounding language of the Christ hymn (Col 1:15-20), in which God is "invisible" and His image is the "firstborn of all creation" (1:15), in whom "all things in heaven and on earth were created" (1:16), also clearly evokes the Jewish Wisdom tradition (cf. Prov 8:22-31),[135] which makes its own claim to Wisdom's relationship to God as "an image of his goodness" (εἰκὼν τῆς ἀγαθότητος αὐτοῦ, eikon tes agathotetos autou, Wis 7:26).

Each of these interpretations naturally take Paul's exaltation of Jesus as the image of God (Col 1:15; cf. 2 Cor 4:4) in a different direction. If it is a challenge to imperial εἰκόνες (images) then Paul is offering Jesus as the one true Lord, over all earthly authorities.[136] If it is a correlation with Genesis 1, then Paul is distinguishing Jesus as the

---

[133] As per Walsh and Keesmaat, *Colossians Remixed*, 66.
[134] This typological connection is similarly argued by Christopher Beetham, *Echoes of Scripture*, 131-32; cf. O'Brien, *Colossians, Philemon*, 43.
[135] Wright argues this carefully in Wright, *Climax of the Covenant*, 108-13; see also Dunn, *Colossians and Philemon*, 88-90; and Sumney, "Writing "In The Image" Of Scripture," in *Paul and Scripture: Extending the Conversation* 198.
[136] Walsh and Keesmaat, *Colossians Remixed*, 163.

exemplary form of humanity according to God's original design.¹³⁷ Or, if Paul is invoking Wisdom, then he is pointing to Jesus as the unique visible form of God Himself (cf. Jn 10:30; 14:9).¹³⁸ In fact, I believe that each of these associations is consciously in play, and that by holding them together they offer a panoramic view of Christ's divine/human identity and the correlative implications for true humanity.

Establishing this requires that we not only study the word εἰκών, but we heed the actions associated with it. As we do, we must keep in view the movement in Paul's overarching anthropological narrative, which identifies Christ as "the image of the invisible God" (Col 1:15) before holding forth the invitation into a renewed humanity "according to the image of its creator" (Col 3:10). Therefore, in this and the following chapters we will consider carefully Paul's use of this evocative term, in comparison with the cultural and religious roots he builds on.

My contention is that while the associations with Wisdom and anti-imperialism contribute to a high Christology, a comparison with Genesis 1 indicates an expressly human dimension, in which the hallmarks of Christ's image identity and the parameters of renewed

---

[137] Wright, *Colossians and Philemon*, 143.
[138] Johnson, "The Image of God in Colossians," *Didaskalia* 10. Cf. Dunn, *Colossians and Philemon*, 88.

humanity exactly match those of the image of God in creation. This serves to develop both an advanced Christology – incorporating both "high" and "low" – and a high anthropology. In this chapter, we will begin examining this by reflecting on Paul's identification of Christ as the image of God.

The firstborn image

As mentioned above, the first reference to the image of God in Colossians is with regard to Christ (Col 1:15). Before we reflect on Paul's application of this eikonic identity to Christ, we should first briefly consider the way he presents it. As noted above, Colossians 1:15-20 is commonly identified as a pre-Pauline, potentially pre-Christian hymn that has been inserted, possibly adapted, to suit Paul's argument.[139] Attempts at reconstructing the original hymn have failed to reach a consensus,[140] as have

---

[139] For pre-Pauline but not pre-Christian see, e.g., Lincoln, *Colossians*, 601-605; for pre-Christian see, e.g., Käsemann, "A Primitive Christian Baptismal Liturgy" in *Essays on New Testament Themes*, 149-68. Opposed to this, Wright has argued that Paul is the sole author and is not interlacing any existing hymnic material: Wright, *Paul: Fresh Perspectives*, 27-28.

[140] How much has been inserted or removed by the author is hotly disputed, causing scholars increasingly to concede that no reliable reconstruction can be reasonably attempted: e.g., Dunn, *Colossians and Philemon*, 84; O'Brien, *Colossians, Philemon,*

Christ, the Image

efforts to trace its use, whether for worshipful praise or credal liturgy.[141] Part of the difficulty lies in its varying theological perspectives, which views creation to be ordered (Col 1:16-17), yet in need of reconciliation (Col 1:20), and Christ to be divine (Col 1:16-17), yet human (Col 1:18). This suggests two voices, and James Dunn has creatively argued that Paul has taken an existing hymn "in praise of Christ's role in creation" (Col 1:15-17) and supplemented it with his own second verse to emphasise "the significance of Christ's redemptive work."[142]

35; Wright, *Colossians and Philemon*, 68. Even at the most basic level, there is disagreement about how the hymn is to be organised. While most argue for a two-strophe structure, dividing into vv.15-17, vv.18-20 (as per Moo, *Colossians and Philemon*, 115; Wright, *Paul: Fresh Perspectives*, 27), some maintain a three-strophe structure, dividing the text into vv.15-16, vv.17-18a, vv.18b-20: e.g., Lincoln, *Colossians*, 602-603; Martin, *Colossians and Philemon*, 55.

[141] For an overview of some of the dominant arguments, see O'Brien, *Colossians, Philemon*, 32-40. For the hymn as worshipful praise see, e.g., Martin, "Aspects of Worship," *Vox Evangelica* 16-17; Arnold, *The Colossian Syncretism*, 247. As such it may have been sung: Thompson, *Colossians and Philemon*, 28. For the hymn as creedal liturgy see, e.g., Eduard Schweizer, *The Letter to the Colossians: A Commentary* (Minneapolis: Augsburg Press, 1982), 51.

[142] Dunn, *Colossians and Philemon*, 85; cf. Arnold, *The Colossian Syncretism*, 249; Martin, *Colossians and Philemon*, 57.

The Colossian Image

Contrary to Eduard Schweizer, who saw theological conflicts between the two voices,[143] I believe Dunn is broadly correct and that Paul is drawing from the Colossians' own worship service and adding to it to show what they have yet to grasp concerning the supremacy of Christ. Specifically, by interweaving a "high" and "low" Christology, Paul affirms that this same Christ they worship as the firstborn of creation (i.e. pre-eminent being) is also the firstborn of the church (i.e. prototype). On this basis, Steve Moyise describes the second strophe of the Christ hymn as one of Paul's most developed "body of Christ" passages.[144]

Thus, at the heart of Paul's overarching message to the Colossians is his exaltation of Christ as one who uniquely shares both deity and humanity. As such, he represents the presence of God among His people and, simultaneously, the perfect vision of true humanity, giving the perfect response to the covenantal call of Israel. Indeed, this binary view of Christ is present throughout Colossians (Col 1:3, 13-14, 27; 2:3, 9-10, 12; 3:1, 4, 15-17), and is a common theme throughout Pauline literature (Rom 4:15, 17-19; 8:29; 1 Cor 1:24, 30; 15:45-49; 2 Cor 3:18; 4:4; Eph 2:15; Phil 2:6, 9-11; 1 Tim 3:16; 6:15-16; Tts 2:3; cf. Heb 1:8-9; 2:17; 4:15).

---

[143] Schweizer, *Colossians*, 44-74.
[144] Moyise, *Paul and Scripture*, 2. Cf. Martin, *Colossians and Philemon*, 55; Barth and Blanke, *Colossians*, 194.

Christ, the Image

This view of Jesus as both master and prototype of humanity, which we might term an advanced Christology, is encapsulated in Paul's claim that "He is the image of the invisible God" (Col 1:15). However, it is striking that this revelation does not stand as the most prominent statement in either the "Christ hymn" or the wider liturgical unit of which it is part, including vv.13-14 (see Fig. I).[145]

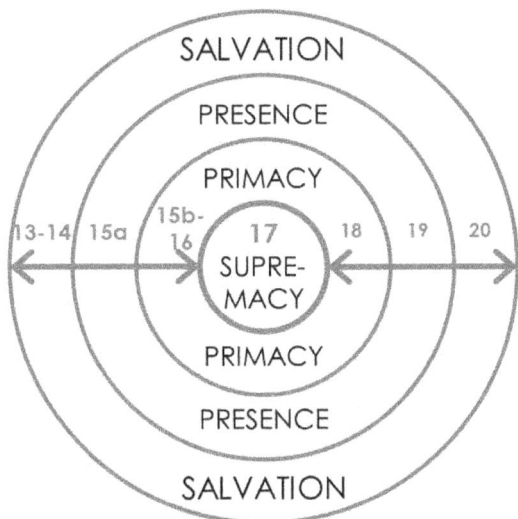

Fig. I – Colossians 1:13-20 chiasmus

---

[145] Markus Barth and Helmut Blanke similarly recognise the importance of attaching these verses to the hymn to form one unit, while also retaining the literary distinction between the introductory creed and the hymn itself: Barth and Blanke, *Colossians*, 194.

By observing this structure we are better placed to look beyond the references that resonate most clearly with us today and see what Paul considered to be the heart of his message. As we particularly consider how this relates to Paul's presentation of humanity, there are three aspects for us to notice.

Firstly, the outer material (vv.13-14, 20) forms an inclusio, which draws on parallel references to the salvation available through Christ to frame the chiasmus and define it as a treatise of restoration. This inclusio describes Jesus taking part in God's rescue mission (1:13), which is further defined as an act of redemption and forgiveness (1:14), and reconciliation (1:20a), and given substance in the explicit reference to the cross (1:20b).[146] The connection between these two verses as the cross-centred outer limits of a systematic unit may potentially be further reinforced by the inclusion in some ancient manuscripts of the phrase "through his blood" to describe the redemption and forgiveness available through Christ, so that the definition of the chiasmus (in meaning and form) is determined by parallel references to Jesus' blood.

We have already seen in chapter three how Paul sets this context of restoration by drawing his readers into the Old Testament narrative, demonstrating that the whole of God's story with His people is located within the person

---

[146] Marianne Meye Thompson also considers this an implicit reference to the cross: Thompson, *Colossians and Philemon*, 27.

of Jesus. Indeed, Jesus represents both sides of the story, God's and Israel's. By positioning this narrative at the entry points to the Christ hymn, then, Paul is inviting the Colossians to find the same restoration in Christ.

Secondly, as we move into the chiasmus, the inner material defines the manner of the restoration. It is here, not in the centre, that we find Paul's assertion of "image" identity, not to diminish it but to position it as the first critical aspect to grasp for understanding Christ's supremacy, both in his divinity and humanity.

As I have stated above, there are a number of possible ways to interpret the significance of εἰκών as Paul's title of choice here, which we will examine more closely in the next three chapters. For now, it is important that we note its correlation within the chiasmus with "the fullness of God" being "pleased to dwell" within him (Col 1:19).[147] As a statement of Christ's divinity, this is a relatively straightforward correlation.[148] More radical is when we attach it to his humanity, which we surely must do if we accept that the thrust of Paul's message is, as Marianne Meye Thompson argues, that "human beings, who are in biblical thought created in God's image, are now also re-

---

[147] Thompson also makes this connection: Thompson, *Colossians and Philemon*, 28.
[148] For examples of how this divinity is applied in this context, see Arnold, *The Colossian Syncretism*, 247; O'Brien, *Colossians, Philemon*, 43.

created in Christ, who is the perfect image of God."[149] For Paul, 'eikonic' identity is connected to the indwelling presence of God.

Following the chiasmus in, we find that this intimate communion is the source of Christ's authority - over both the cosmos (Col 1:15b) and the church (Col 1:18a, c) - and of his life-giving power (Col 1:16 cf. 1:18b). These, as we have already observed in chapter two, are the very hallmarks of true humanity that Paul portrays throughout his letter to the Colossians.

Finally we reach the vertex, which declares the absolute supremacy of Christ (Col 1:17). On the basis of his redemptive place in both God's and humanity's story, on the basis of his intimate communion with God, both as the divine Son and the human Christ, and the power and authority this endows him with, Jesus is before all things. Having reached this central position of primacy, we can then look backwards to his place as "firstborn of all creation" (Col 1:15b) and forwards to his place as "firstborn from the dead" (Col 1:18) – testifying to his highest status in the creation and the re-creation – to see how the whole of God's person, purposes and power are located in Christ, His image.

---

[149] Thompson, *Colossians and Philemon*, 29.

Chapter Seven
IMAGE AND EMPIRE

Having seen how Paul uses "image" to define his Christology, we must now consider the implications of this language for true humanity. To do this, we must first reflect on how εἰκών would have resonated as a religious and cultural calling-card both for Paul as author, and the Colossians as readers. Our first point of consideration is its significance in terms of Paul's and Colossae's context within the Roman Empire, with which Paul claimed at least some association (Acts 22:25-29), especially connected to the prevalence of the imperial cult.

As far back as 1908, Adolf Deissmann argued that early Christianity developed a "polemical parallelism between the cult of the emperor and the cult of Christ,"[150] evidenced in the letters of Paul by his conscious use of imperial vocabulary, including εὐαγγέλιον (euaggelion, "good news"), παρουσία (parousia, "presence" or "coming"), and ἐπιφάνεια (epiphaneia, "appearance"), and

---

[150] Deissmann, *Light from the Ancient East*, 346.

most particularly by his provocative ascription to Jesus of titles reserved for the emperor, such as θεοῦ υἱός (theou huios, "son of God"), κύριος (kyrios, "lord"), βασιλεύς (basileus, "king"), σωτήρ (soter, "saviour") and ἀρχιερεύς (archiereus, "high priest"),[151] so-used because Paul "was bound to protest against the adornment of any other with the sacred formula."[152] It is only in more recent years, however, that there has been a growing call from some scholars for readers of Paul to recognise not only his Jewish context, but his place within Roman imperial history.[153]

Klaus Wengst, Dieter Georgi, Richard Horsley and N. T. Wright have all been influential proponents of this approach,[154] which is well summarised by Harry Maier, in his discussion of the pastoral epistles, when he asserts that "reading these letters with the help of imperial imagery and with a view to imperial language is indispensable for an understanding of the epistles' social context,

---

[151] Deissmann, *Light from the Ancient East*, 347-78; see also Barclay, *Pauline Churches and Diaspora Jews*, 364.
[152] Deissmann, *Light from the Ancient East*, 350.
[153] Barclay, *Pauline Churches and Diaspora Jews*, 363.
[154] E.g., see Wengst, *Pax Romana and the Presence of Jesus Christ* ; Georgi, *Theocracy In Paul's Practice and Theology* ; Horsley, *Paul and Empire* ; Wright, *Paul: Fresh Perspectives*, 69-79; also Wright, "Paul's Gospel and Caesar's Empire" in *Paul and Politics: Ekklesia, Israel, Imperium, Interpretation: Essays in Honour of Krister Stendahl*.

vocabulary and metaphor, strategies of persuasion and communal ideals."[155] This position is readily defended with archaeological evidence that points to an imperial cult that had embedded itself quickly across the empire and become firmly established by the time of Paul's writing.

Altars and temples, law courts and theatres, statues and triumphal arches filled the Romanized world,[156] bearing the "image" and proclaiming the lordship of Caesar, who was both "saviour and the incarnation of divine good news for the whole world."[157] Around this was built a society that worshipped its emperor, who had, after all, brought peace (Pax Romana) and prosperity through his divine rule.[158] Most notably for this study, these proclamations were put into the hands of all subjects through the institution of currency, with coins bearing the "image" of Caesar.[159] It is therefore significant that the only instances of εἰκών used in the Gospels come from the synoptic accounts of Jesus subverting the Pharisees' attempt to trap him with a question concerning tax.

---

[155] Maier, *Picturing Paul in Empire*, 1.
[156] Horsley, *Paul and Empire*, 73-74; Marcus, "Idolatry in the New Testament," *Interpretation* 156; Maier, "A Sly Civility," *Journal for the Study of the New Testament* 326.
[157] Gorman, *Apostle of the Crucified Lord*, 9, 11.
[158] Gorman, *Apostle of the Crucified Lord*, 9-11.
[159] Gorman, *Apostle of the Crucified Lord*, 17; Maier, *Picturing Paul in Empire*, 9.

"Whose head [εἰκών] is this, and whose title?" he asks them (Mt 22:20; Mk 12:16; cf. Lk 20:24). The inscription or "title" (ἐπιγραφή, epigraphe) on the denarius in question (Mt 22:19; Mk 12:15; Lk 20:24), assuming it is from the Tiberias mint, declares Caesar to be both 'Pontif Maxim' ("high priest") and 'Ti[berivs] Caesar Divi Avg[vsti] F[ilivs] Avgvstvs' – "Tiberias Caesar, son of the deified Augustus" (see Fig. J).[160]

Fig. J – Tiberius denarius

In response to this, Richard Horsley claims, "Paul deliberately used language closely associated with the imperial religion [to present] his gospel as a direct competitor of the gospel of Caesar."[161] Looking back to the words identified by Adolf Deissmann, it is striking

---

[160] Marcus, *Idolatry in the New Testament*, 156.
[161] Horsley, *Paul and Empire*, 140; cf. Walsh and Keesmaat, *Colossians Remixed*, 66.

that Paul makes frequent use of κύριος in Colossians (Col 1:3,10; 2:6; 3:13, 17, 18, 20, 22, 23, 24; 4:1, 7, 17),[162] emphasising, as N. T. Wright observes, that "for Paul, Jesus is Lord and Caesar is not."[163] There are also repeated references to the sonship of Christ (1:3, 13; 3:6)[164] and εὐαγγέλιον (euaggelion, "good news," 1:5, 23).

Maier extrapolates this view of εὐαγγέλιον to forge a link between the fruitfulness Paul describes (Col 1:6, 10) and the "natural abundance and earthly fertility" that Caesar was celebrated to manifest.[165] To this, he adds ἀποκαταλλάσσω (apokatallasso, "reconcile," Col 1:20, 22) and εἰρηνοποιέω/εἰρήνη (eireopoieo/eirene, "make peace"/"peace," Col 1:20 / 1:2; 3:15).[166] He also specifies the significance of the triumph over rulers described in Colossians 2:15 (which itself echoes Christ's authority over the dominions, rulers and powers in Col 1:16) as a lynchpin anti-imperial claim.[167]

Interestingly, despite the link to coins made in the Gospels mentioned above, neither Adolf Deissmann nor

---

[162] Indeed, this is a regular feature of the Pauline corpus. In Romans alone it is used thirty-two times, and just as frequently elsewhere.
[163] Wright, *Paul: Fresh Perspectives*, 69.
[164] Used nineteen times in the Pauline corpus.
[165] Maier, *A Sly Civility*, 334.
[166] Maier, *A Sly Civility*, 326.
[167] Maier, *A Sly Civility*, 326, 332-22; cf. Arnold, *The Colossian Syncretism*, 281.

The Colossian Image

Harry Maier suggest that εἰκών carries counter-imperial connotations. Brian Walsh and Sylvia Keesmaat do, however, arguing that "as soon as he [Paul] made references to 'image of God,' 'firstborn' and 'first place,' everyone with ears to hear would know that he was contrasting Jesus with Caesar."[168] For them, the issue Paul is confronting is idolatry, and their logic is compelling. Humans were made to bear God's image, but if they choose not to, "this does not mean we are no longer image-bearers. Rather ... we will find something [else] in the creation to serve as our god."[169]

At this point, however, the word study breaks down, as we must concede that Colossians makes no mention of βασιλεύς (basileus, "king"),[170] σωτήρ (soter, "saviour"),[171] ἀρχιερεύς (archierius, "high priest"),[172] παρουσία (parousia,

---

[168] Walsh and Keesmaat, *Colossians Remixed*, 89.
[169] Walsh and Keesmaat, *Colossians Remixed*, 163.
[170] Which is in fact only used in the Pauline corpus in 1 Tim 1:17 and 6:15, being more commonly used in the Gospels and Revelation.
[171] Also not a common term for Paul, mentioned in Eph 5:23; Phil 3:20; 1 Tim 1:1; 2:3; 4:10; and 2 Tim 1:10. That is, until Titus, where it is used as a major theme and features six times (1:3, 4; 2:10, 13; 3:4, 6).
[172] This is never used by Paul, but is very common in Hebrews (2:17; 3:1; 4:14, 15; 5:1, 5, 10; 6:20; 7:26, 27, 28; 8:1, 3; 9:7, 11; 13:11).

"coming"),¹⁷³ or ἐπιφάνεια (epiphaneia, "appearance")¹⁷⁴ It is also notable that despite its frequency in Colossians, κύριος (kyrios, "lord") does not feature in the Christ hymn, which is surely the perfect place to emphasise lordship over Caesar, as Christ's authority over all thrones, dominions, rulers and powers is declared (v.16), and he is exalted as the divine image (v.15) in place of the emperor.

Instead, κύριος is used ambiguously in places, such that it could be referring to Jesus or to the LORD God (i.e. Yahweh), commensurate with its use in the LXX.¹⁷⁵ Of particular note is the Lord's role in the divine process of forgiveness (Col 3:13), the divine inspiration of fear (3:22), and the divine gift of inheritance (3:24). Throughout Scripture, these are taken to be signposts to God,¹⁷⁶ and it seems likely that Paul's frequent use of κύριος is principally concerned with associating the Son with the Father, rather than the liberator Christ against the oppressor Caesar, even if that inevitably stands as a significant yet supplementary implication.

---

[173] Used eight times in the Pauline corpus.
[174] Used six times in the Pauline corpus, and nowhere else in the NT.
[175] This is also true of Paul's use in Romans. For example, Rom 4:8; 9:28; 11:34; 12:11, 19; 14:11; 15:11 may refer to God, whereas the scriptural quotes in Rom 9:29; 10:16, and 11:3 certainly do.
[176] For forgiveness, see e.g., Ps 130:4, Lk 5:20-21, 23:34; for fear, see e.g., Deut 10:12, Job 28:28, Lk 21:26; for inheritance, see e.g., Num 33:54, Jos 1:6, Jer 3:18, Mic 2:4; Mt 21:38.

The Colossian Image

We might also observe that the use of εἰρηνοποιέω ("make peace") is the only instance of this word in the whole New Testament. That said, εἰρήνη (eirene, "peace") as a more general term is used frequently,[177] strikingly in Ephesians 2:15, when it is again used in conjunction with ἀποκαταλλάσσω (apokatallasso, "reconcile," Eph 2:16) to create a new humanity:

> He has abolished the law with its commandments and ordinances, that he might create in himself one new humanity in place of the two, thus making peace [εἰρήνην], and might reconcile [ἀποκαταλλάξῃ] both groups to God in one body through the cross, thus putting to death that hostility through it.
>
> Ephesians 2:15-16

This may cast doubt on the argument that the language used in Colossians relates to a wider polemic against empire. In fact, it is far from a unanimous view that Paul confronts Rome in Colossians at all. Ralph Martin sees Paul's language as carefully chosen to evoke Jewish, not imperial thoughts.[178] Robert Wall argues similarly, but

---

[177] Used thirty-eight times in the Pauline corpus outside of Colossians, including ten uses in Romans alone (Rom 1:7; 2:10; 3:17; 5:1; 8:6; 14:17, 19; 15:13, 33; 16:20).
[178] Martin, *Colossians and Philemon*, 55-57.

Image and Empire

presses the importance of Hellenised thinking, specifically identifying Platonic undertones to Paul's portrayal of Christ as the visible image of the invisible God (Col 1:15).[179] Whereas Clinton Arnold finds close connections between Paul's language in the Christ hymn (1:15-20) and the traditional Jewish understanding about angelic and demonic powers,[180] concluding that the whole letter is a carefully worded rhetoric against the Colossian philosophy.[181] While the arguments made in these cases have much going for them, we must be careful not to underestimate the imperial significance of Paul's language. Here we may follow the examples of Harry Maier and Morna Hooker, who in their respective arguments for Paul's imperial and Jewish intentions, both

---

[179] Wall, *Colossians and Philemon*, 64-66; cf. Lohse, *Colossians and Philemon*, 47; Dunn, *Colossians and Philemon*, 87; this is dismissed by O'Brien: O'Brien, *Colossians, Philemon*, 43.

[180] In particular, Paul's reference to "thrones or dominions or rulers or powers" (Col 1:16) represent four terms used specifically of angelic hosts and powers in Jewish literature. Regarding "thrones" see 2 En 20:1; TLev 3:8; TAb 13:10; TSol 3:5. Regarding "dominions" see 1 En 61:10; 2 En 20:1; CavTre 1:3; TSol 8:6. Regarding "rulers" see Rom 8:38 (Paul's only other use of this word, and it is in connection with angels); 1 En 6:7-8; TAb 13:10. Regarding "powers" see Eph 2:2 (used of Satan); 1 Pet 3:22; 3 Bar 12:3; TLev 3:8; TAb 13:10.

[181] Arnold, *The Colossian Syncretism*, 251-55. We will discuss this further in chapter twelve.

concede that the alternative interpretation cannot be ignored.[182]

Perhaps the most reasonable view is a combination of Joel Marcus' submission that Paul confronts paganism and idolatry more generally,[183] with Richard Horsley's caveat that, "The imperial cult rapidly became the most widespread of all cults."[184] Taken together, this has the effect of elevating Christ whilst flattening all pretenders to the same level, separating the potential influences over the Church into two categories: Christ, in whom they may attain true humanity, and all others, in whom they will not. John Barclay puts it thus: "Paul's most subversive act, vis-à-vis the Roman empire, was not to oppose or upstage it, but to relegate it to the rank of a dependent and derivative entity, denied a distinguishable name or significant role in the story of the world."[185]

---

[182] Hooker says, "Paul did not derive these titles from Rome, for they came into Christian usage from the Old Testament, but such terms would have rung bells in the minds of his converts. The Christian gospel was inevitably seen as a challenge to the imperial cult." Hooker, *Paul*, 38; cf. Maier, *A Sly Civility*, 329, 333.
[183] Marcus, *Idolatry in the New Testament*, 153-54; cf. Barclay, *Pauline Churches and Diaspora Jews*, 363-88; and Ziesler, *Pauline Christianity*, 35-36.
[184] Horsley, *Paul and Empire*, 72.
[185] Barclay, *Pauline Churches and Diaspora Jews*, 383-84; cf. Wright, *Paul and the Faithfulness of God*, 1286, 1307-08.

Image and Empire

Where we must direct our attention, then, is on the implications this confrontation of empire may have for Christ's identity as the true image of God. His 'eikonic' status is a declaration of his sovereignty, divinity, and high priesthood, rooted in his communion with God, and displayed in his authority and life-giving power. N. T. Wright calls this "Christological monotheism."[186] Christ is not a new god to be worshipped in a neo-Christian pantheon, but is the embodiment of Yahweh, the One God of the Covenant. Crucially, though, this is not a status he carries for self-glorification, but for the blessing of creation and humanity. Christ stands as the true image that inspires humanity to its own greater status in a way the Pax Romana or the empty promises of pagan idols never could.

---

[186] Wright, *Climax of the Covenant*, 99.

Chapter Eight

IMAGE AND WISDOM

Turning now from the cultural significance of εἰκών to its spiritual, or more accurately, Scriptural importance, it would perhaps be surprising for the casual reader of the Christ hymn (1:15-20), specifically its identification of Jesus as "the image of the invisible God" (1:15), to discover that the biblical allusion most widely acknowledged among recent scholars is not to Genesis 1:26-28, but to the personification of Wisdom in Proverbs 8:22-31:

> When he [God] established the heavens I [Wisdom] was there ... when he marked out the foundations of the earth, then I was beside him, like a master worker.
> Proverbs 8:27a, 29b-30

The link to Genesis certainly is recognised,[187] and we shall assess it below, but Peter O'Brien reflects well the popular

---

[187] E.g., see Thompson, *Colossians and Philemon*, 28-29; O'Brien, *Colossians, Philemon*, 43.

view that "Genesis 1 alone does not adequately explain the background to [the image] ... Paul, in common with other NT writers, identified Christ with the Wisdom of God."[188] For the most part, then, any correlation with Genesis 1:26-28 is considered an echo in comparison to the more explicit allusion to Wisdom.[189]

A quick reading of Proverbs 8 is sufficient to see much of the reasoning behind this connection. Wisdom is born first in creation (Prov 8:22, 24 cf. Col 1:15b), there at the beginning (ἀρχή, arche, Prov 8:22, 23 cf. Col 1:18). Not that she is a created being, as the third-fourth century Christian heretic Arius concluded,[190] but that she is the pre-existent agent of creation, participating as a "master worker" (Prov 8:30 cf. Col 1:16). There is therefore a clear conceptual overlap between Proverbs 8 and Colossians 1:15-17, which appears to include vocabulary that would naturally have evoked Wisdom ideas in Paul's readers.

However, given this apparent correlation, and that this is one of the few examples of a personified-Wisdom tradition in the Old Testament, it seems remarkable that

---

[188] O'Brien, *Colossians, Philemon*, 43
[189] E.g., Barclay, *Colossians and Philemon*, 67; Wright, *Colossians and Philemon*, 71-72; Dunn, *Colossians and Philemon*, 86-90; Lincoln, *Colossians*, 597; Thompson, *Colossians and Philemon*, 29; Moo, *Colossians and Philemon*, 118-20.
[190] As confronted by the early Church Father Athanasius in his *Against the Arians*, 2.16.18-24.

Image and Wisdom

Proverbs makes no mention of "image," despite its importance in Colossians, and Barrett's claim that "image is a word that belongs to the Wisdom literature."[191] This inference is drawn from its use elsewhere, most notably Wisdom of Solomon 7:26: "She [Wisdom] is the perfect image of God's goodness."[192] This is reinforced further when we connect Wisdom and Logos theologies, which James Dunn and Douglas Moo both consider in essence interchangeable,[193] representative as they both are of God's Word spoken through Creation and Torah. Philo unpacks the Jewish view of Logos extensively and in so doing makes a number of references to εἰκών, often as the one who makes the invisible God visible (*De confusione linguarum*, 97, 147; *De fuga et invention*, 101; *De somnis*, 1.239 cf. *De somnis*, 2.45).

Despite its popularity, this view is not universal. Gordon Fee is among the most vocal and careful critics, and it is worth noting his objections. These can be condensed into two issues. Firstly, that two of the four terms usually advanced as evidence of Wisdom – πρωτότοκος (prototokos, "firstborn," Col 1:15, 18) and πρὸ πάντων (pro panton, "before all things," Col 1:17) – do not feature anywhere else in Wisdom literature, while the other two

---

[191] Barrett, *Paul*, 146-47.
[192] Dunn, *Colossians and Philemon*, 88.
[193] Dunn, *Colossians and Philemon*, 88; Moo, *Colossians and Philemon*, 118.

– ἀρχή (arche, "beginning," Col 1:18) and εἰκών (eikon, "image," Col 1:15) – only feature once apiece (Prov 8:23 and Wis 7:26 respectively).[194]

Secondly, Paul's use of σοφία (Col 1:9, 28; 2:3, 23; 3:16; 4:5) neither features within the claimed appeal to Wisdom (Col 1:15-20), nor is it ever used to imply personified Wisdom but "the attribute of wisdom."[195] Instead, the emphasis on reconciling creation as Christ's ultimate purpose (something Ralph Martin acknowledges is never a feature of Jewish wisdom theology)[196] sets Paul's image language within the context of Creation and therefore this is, after all, a direct reference to Genesis 1.[197] Building on Martin's observation that reconciling Creation is consistently absent from Wisdom theology, we might add that the reconciliation of humanity described in the second strophe of the Christ hymn, which is later reimagined in terms of a new humanity, renewed in the image of the Creator (Col 3:10), also seems out of place in a Wisdom text. Whereas it fits perfectly in a creation-centric text, which proclaims an Adam Christology in addition to affirming Christ's divine nature.[198]

---

[194] Fee, *Pauline Christology*, 319-25.
[195] Fee, *Pauline Christology*, 318.
[196] Martin, *Colossians and Philemon*, 58.
[197] Fee, *Pauline Christology*, 325; cf. Moo, *Colossians and Philemon*, 119.
[198] O'Brien, *Colossians, Philemon*, 190-91; Dunn, *Colossians and Philemon*, 221-22; Wall, *Colossians and Philemon*, 142.

Image and Wisdom

Nevertheless, I would not press as far as Fee in rejecting altogether the correlation with the Jewish Wisdom tradition. After all, it is not only the intent of the author that we need to assess, but the mind-set of the reader, and it seems unlikely that the undertones of Wisdom would go unnoticed by either. Instead, I would reposition it, similarly to N. T. Wright,[199] within Paul's wider covenantal, restorative theology. I am therefore inclined to view Paul's use of εἰκών, and its surrounding language, not as an *allusion* to Wisdom and an *echo* of creation, but the other way around.

Certainly, Paul must have been aware of the way this Old Testament language had developed within the recent theology of his day, and therefore how it would be heard by his readers, and that is precisely the reason to use it. The effect of this association with Wisdom is the elevation of Christ to the highest place in creation. He is pre-existent and, therefore, pre-eminent over all thrones, dominions, rulers and powers (Col 1:16), for such authority is bestowed upon the kings of the world by their creator, whereas Paul's claim here is that Christ's authority is not given, it is inherent to his very nature. He *is* the Creator, the "master worker" (Prov 8:30), distinct in his identity as the Son, yet inseparable from the Father,[200] God Himself. As Martin puts it, "Christ as God's image

---

[199] Wright, *Climax of the Covenant*, 115-17.
[200] Wright, *Colossians and Philemon*, 73.

means that he is not a copy of God, 'like him'; he is the objectivization of God in human life, the 'projection' of God on the canvas of our humanity, and the embodiment of the divine in the world of men."[201]

---

[201] Martin, *Colossians and Philemon*, 57.

Chapter Nine

IMAGE AND CREATION

Each of the aforementioned connotations of εἰκών, relating to Empire and Wisdom, are compelling and shed important light on Paul's Christological intentions. However, while his challenge to the imperial cult emphasises Christ's heavenly sovereignty, and Wisdom his heavenly agency (and, therefore, both attest to his divinity), neither satisfactorily expresses his humanity. Yet the human nature of Christ is an essential aspect of Paul's Christology in general (e.g. Rom 1:3; 5:15-19; Gal 4:4; Phil 2:7; 1 Tim 2:5),[202] and the Christ hymn in particular (Col 1:18).[203] Moreover, although strong arguments have been put forward to pinpoint the use of "image" language as rooted in both Empire and Wisdom, in fact in each instance this largely relies on building a case from the hymn that surrounds the "image" more than the presentation of the "image" itself.

---

[202] Note also his mortality asserted in Galatians 3:1, Philippians 2:9, Colossians 2:13 and 1 Thessalonians 2:15.
[203] Thompson, *Colossians and Philemon*, 28-29.

The Colossian Image

For all the effort to show a creative diversity to Paul's use of image, successfully and appositely as we have seen, we must concede, with Johnson, that "in the case of the 'image of God' in Colossians the particular biblical text which most informs the term is Genesis 1:24-30."[204] Indeed, this link seems to be at the heart of the Wisdom and Logos traditions we have briefly examined,[205] with several texts describing Wisdom/Logos in the context of creation (Prov 8:22-30; Wis 7:22; 8:6; Sir 24:4-5; and in Philo: *De somnis*, 1.239; 2.45). N. T. Wright even describes the Wisdom tradition as a form of Creation theology.[206] The pattern of Wisdom/Logos literature is also to describe humanity, not Wisdom, as the image of God (Wis 2:23; Sir 17:3; 2 Esd 8:44). Perhaps most explicit is Philo's portrayal of Wisdom within the context of creation in a manner that echoes not only the sixth day of Genesis 1, but the fourth day as well:

---

[204] Johnson, *The Image of God in Colossians*, 9; cf. Wright, *Paul: Fresh Perspectives*, 27; Middleton, *A New Heaven And A New Earth*, 166; Thiselton, *The Living Paul*, 67; Peterson, "The Image of God in Pauline Preaching," *Leaven* 2; Arnold, *The Colossian Syncretism*, 249.

[205] Murphy and Carm, "Wisdom and Creation," *Journal of Biblical Literature* 4.

[206] Wright, *Paul and the Faithfulness of God*, 670; cf. Murphy and Carm, "Wisdom and Creation," *Journal of Biblical Literature* 4.

Image and Creation

> For just as those who are unable to see the sun itself see the gleam of the parhelion and take it for the sun, and take the halo around the moon for that luminary itself, so some regard the image of God, His angel the Word, as His very self.
>
> Philo, De somnis, 1.239

Creation is also the explicit setting of the Christ hymn. Christ's image identity is coupled with his being "the firstborn of all creation" (Col 1:16). Despite this, Steve Moyise asserts that Paul's "only quotation from the creation stories comes in 2 Corinthians 4:6."[207] This is peculiar, since although the passage clearly alludes to Genesis 1:3, the source he cites, it is not a direct quotation. Paul writes, "For it is the God who said, 'Let light shine out of darkness' ..." (ὅτι ὁ θεὸς ὁ εἰπών, Ἐκ σκότους φῶς λάμψει ..., oti o theos o eipon, Ek skotous phos lampsei ..., 2 Cor 4:6) whereas Genesis 1:3 in the LXX reads: καὶ εἶπεν ὁ θεός γενηθήτω φῶς (kai eipen o theos genetheto phos). It is therefore remarkable that he does not equally recognise Colossians 1:15 (or indeed 2 Corinthians 4:4) as relating to Genesis 1:27, given the closer correspondence between εἰκὼν τοῦ θεοῦ (eikon tou theou, Col 1:15; 2 Cor 4:4) and εἰκόνα θεοῦ (eikona theou, Gen 1:27, LXX). This association would surely have

---

[207] Moyise, *Paul and Scripture*, 16.

resonated as powerfully with Paul's original readers as it does today, and so to reduce it to an echo instead of a strong allusion is to underestimate Paul's intentions to form his Christological vision around not only Christ's heavenly agency, but also his true humanity.

Proceeding on the basis that Colossians 1:15 is a strong allusion to Genesis 1:27, the question arises how far to press this connection. Is it only to evoke a theological framework, i.e. to place Christ within a cosmological scheme, or does it also highlight a deeper truth about the quality of Christ's human nature? A brief analysis of Genesis 1:26-28 may be helpful here:

> Then God said, "Let us make humankind in our image, according to our likeness; and let them have dominion over the fish of the sea, and over the birds of the air, and over the cattle, and over all the wild animals of the earth, and over every creeping thing that creeps upon the earth." So God created humankind in his image, in the image of God he created them; male and female he created them. God blessed them, and God said to them, "Be fruitful and multiply, and fill the earth and subdue it; and have dominion over the fish of the sea and over the birds of the air and over every living thing that moves upon the earth."
> Genesis 1:26-28

Image and Creation

Before we begin to examine this text, in the hope of better understanding it, we must first recognise that this is no small task. Theologians have debated the meaning of the image of God in Genesis for centuries,[208] and the task is made all the more complicated by the fact that Genesis 1 is notoriously obscure about the precise nature of the image.[209] Consequently, the discussion has veered away from what the image *is* to what the image *does*.[210]

In the main, three observations have been made. Firstly, there is a special *relationship* established between God and humanity,[211] His image (צֶלֶם, tselem, Gen 1:26).[212] This suggests a degree of similarity between God and His

---

[208] It is actively discussed by the patristics, but even this is late in the debate, given the focus of this study showing Paul sparking this discussion among Christian communities, and the Wisdom and Logos theologies we have already considered from Judaism. This is discussed in greater detail by Van Wolde and Middleton: Van Wolde, *Stories of the Beginning*, 25; Middleton, *The Liberating Image*, 18-21.

[209] Wenham, *Genesis 1-15*, 32; Van Wolde, *Stories of the Beginning*, 25; Hamilton, *Genesis 1-17*, 137.

[210] Brueggemann, *Genesis*, 33; Turner, *Genesis*, 14; Johnson, *The Image of God in Colossians*, 10; Middleton, *The Liberating Image*, 27.

[211] Hamilton, *Genesis 1-17*, 137.

[212] Van Wolde says of צֶלֶם (tselem) that it is "a general word which denotes a relationship:" Van Wolde, *Stories of the Beginning*, 27. However, as we shall see, it can be argued that there is rather more to it than that.

image,²¹³ which enables humanity to hear from, and to speak to God.²¹⁴ Indeed, the specific correlation between God's and humanity's "sensory abilities" has been studied in detail by Yael Avrahami, who argues that what marks humanity in Genesis 1:26-27 out against false idols is its ability to see, hear, speak, eat, breathe, smell, touch and walk as God does.²¹⁵ This connection brings with it the responsibility to represent Him in the world, even as it marks humanity as distinct from the rest of creation,²¹⁶ since it is the only species designed to conform to God, and not "their own kind" (Gen 1:20, 24).²¹⁷

Secondly, with the commission to "have dominion" (Gen 1:26) and "fill the earth and subdue it" (Gen 1:28), God's image is bestowed with the *authority* to rule and subdue creation.²¹⁸ It is almost unanimously acknowledged now that צֶלֶם (tselem, "image") evokes a royal status.²¹⁹ Kings in Egypt and the Near East were called the "image of god" and seen to be agents of divine

---

²¹³ Turner, *Genesis*, 22.
²¹⁴ Wenham, *Genesis 1-15*, 31; Thiselton, *The Living Paul*, 67; Barth, *Church Dogmatics III.I*, 183-87; 196.
²¹⁵ Avrahami, *The Senses of Scripture*, 65-112, 189-222.
²¹⁶ Turner, *Genesis*, 15.
²¹⁷ Van Wolde, *Stories of the Beginning*, 24.
²¹⁸ E.g., Thiselton, *The Living Paul*, 67; Johnson, *The Image of God in Colossians*, 1; Turner calls this, "the major way in which human activity reflects the divine." Turner, *Genesis*, 14.
²¹⁹ Middleton, *The Liberating Image*, 26, 51.

will.²²⁰ They in turn would set up images of themselves across their kingdom to represent them in their absence.²²¹ In short, to be an image of God was to be given "a mandate of power and responsibility. But it is power exercised as God exercises power."²²²

Contrary to the way humans tend to subdue, this does not permit humanity to become tyrants over creation (cf. Num 32:22, 29; Jos 18:1; 2 Chr 28:10; Neh 5:5; Est 7:8; Jer 34:11). Rather, as Adam was put in the garden to "till it and keep it" (Gen 2:15), and in line with the tradition of shepherd kings (Eze 34), theirs is to be a rule of care. This is what God expects of them in the Levitical Law (Lev 25), and how the king is portrayed in Psalm 72.²²³ With this in mind, J. Richard Middleton observes that while כָּבַשׁ (kabas, "subdue") is often used in a context of violence between people, within a context of agriculture, which is the setting of this passage as humanity is given dominion over the land and animals (not on another), "there is no implication of a violent adversarial relationship to the land/earth per se."²²⁴

---

[220] Wenham, *Genesis 1-15*, 30; Hamilton, *Genesis 1-17*, 135.
[221] Brueggemann, *Genesis*, 32, 35; Von Rad, *Genesis*, 60.
[222] Brueggemann, *Genesis*, 32; cf. Middleton, *The Liberating Image*, 27.
[223] Hamilton, *Genesis 1-17*, 138-39; cf. Van Wolde, *Stories of the Beginning*, 30-31.
[224] Middleton, *The Liberating Image*, 52.

Finally, there is an *equality* within humanity. This is displayed in two directions: i) Despite the authority God bestows on His image being royal in character, it is not restricted to political rulers or a social elite but is given to the whole of humanity, regardless of earthly power, status, or ethnicity.[225] This democratisation of humanity stands in stark contrast to the social structures of Israel's neighbours; ii) God's image is created to be male and female. This picture of equality in community is fundamental to the image identity. Only when taken together do men and women (plural) become the image of God (singular), because it is only in unity and community that humanity reflects God,[226] who, it appears from the use of the first person plural pronouns "us" and "our" (Gen 1:26), is Himself a community.[227]

Each of these three common observations may be categorised as hallmarks of the image. Before moving on, though, I want to draw attention to two other aspects that have tended to escape the mainstream discussion of this matter: one because it is underestimated, the other because it has not yet had time to become established.

---

[225] Wenham, *Genesis 1-15*, 31; cf. Hamilton, *Genesis 1-17*, 135.
[226] Brueggemann, *Genesis*, 34.
[227] There is much debate over this, and many other suggestions than this, but as Victor Hamilton argues, this must be considered a reasonable Christian interpretation: Hamilton, *Genesis 1-17*, 133-34.

Firstly, I suggest that we must acknowledge a fourth hallmark, in the form of humanity's commission to "be fruitful and multiply, and fill the earth" (Gen 1:28). Besides a passing mention of its presence, this aspect has tended to be overlooked by interpreters, who have dismissed it as a blessing of no special concern, since it is one shared with all other life.[228] Instead, attention has been directed either towards humanity's relationship with God or towards its authority in creation.[229]

However, as Victor Hamilton notes, the identification of humanity as male and female is as much a statement of function as substance, and points to their calling to procreate.[230] This is reinforced by J. Richard Middleton's assertion that זָכָר (zakar, "male") and נְקֵבָה (neqebah, "female") are biological terms, as opposed to the social terms of אִישׁ (ish, "man") and אִשָּׁה (ishah, "woman").[231] We should also note the great distinction between the way humanity and the rest of life fulfils their commission to fruitfulness. Where it is governed by inherency in the plants and instinct in the animals, it is uniquely a choice in humanity, a mark of their relationship with God. In one of the few treatments of this side of human nature, Claus Westermann speaks of this as a theology of blessing,

---

[228] Turner, *Genesis*, 14; Van Wolde, *Stories of the Beginning*, 30.
[229] Wenham, *Genesis 1-15*, 33.
[230] Hamilton, *Genesis 1-17*, 139.
[231] Middleton, *The Liberating Image*, 50.

which points to the "generative power or life, fertility and well-being that God has ordained within the normal flow and mystery of life."²³² Something Walter Brueggemann has called "God's life-giving work."²³³

Lastly, we must revisit the hallmark of relationship. Naturally an important aspect of the discussion regarding humanity's image identity has centred on the meaning of צֶלֶם (tselem, "image"). It has long been recognised by scholars that a more common use of this term is for an idol, or cult statue (Num 33:52; 2 Kgs 11:18; 2 Chr 23:17; Eze 7:20; 16:17; Am 5:26).²³⁴ However, this correlation carries such negative connotations that interpretations in the Church have tended towards a more comfortable view of "image" that is more akin to "likeness."²³⁵ Bucking this trend, Gordon Wenham looked beyond the negative associations of false idols to the intended function of them and concluded that "divine spirit was often thought of as

---

²³² Cited by Brueggemann, from Westerman, *Blessing in the Bible and the Life of the Church* . See Brueggemann, *Genesis*, 37.
²³³ Brueggemann, *Genesis*, 37.
²³⁴ Hamilton, *Genesis 1-17*, 134; Middleton, *The Liberating Image*, 25, 45.
²³⁵ Derek Kidner, *Genesis: An Introduction and Commentary* (Leicester: Inter Varsity Press, 1967), 50-51; cf. David Atkinson, *The Message of Genesis 1-11* (Leicester: Inter Varsity Press, 1990), 36-37.

indwelling an idol."²³⁶ Crispin Fletcher-Louis has pressed this further to claim that this is the primary meaning of צֶלֶם in Genesis 1,²³⁷ on the basis that "an idol is set up in a sacred place or building to be the real presence of and visible form of the god."²³⁸

This has two startling implications for humanity. Firstly, it brings to mind temple imagery. "No pagan temple could be complete," says J. Richard Middleton, "without the installation of the cult image of the deity."²³⁹ Similarly, the cosmos has been created as the ultimate temple, with God's perfect image set up within, representing him and reflecting him to the world. But also, within this temple, humanity carries a priestly role to mediate the presence of God to the world (cf. Ex 19:6; 1 Pet 2:9), only they do it not through ritual but through living lives devoted to God, which then resonate His holy presence. This takes us out of the realm of what the image *does* and back into what it *is*. It is the dwelling place of God on earth, the house from which he rules (cf. 2 Chr 7:12).²⁴⁰

---

[236] Wenham, *Genesis 1-15*, 31.
[237] Fletcher-Louis, "God's Image, Temple and High Priest," in *Heaven on Earth: The Temple in Biblical Theology* 83.
[238] Fletcher-Louis, "God's Image, Temple and High Priest," in *Heaven on Earth: The Temple in Biblical Theology* 84.
[239] Middleton, *The Liberating Image*, 87.
[240] Cf. Middleton, *A New Heaven And A New Earth*, 166.

The Colossian Image

Taking these hallmarks all together, then, the image of God in Genesis offers an extraordinary vision for humanity: sharing an intimate communion of indwelling presence with God, bearing His authority in ruling over creation, exercising that authority by life-giving power and fruitfulness, and living as a united people (See Fig. K). These are the very same things we have watched God doing through the first six days of creation, and so as humanity steps up to the mark, it reflects, represents and resonates God to the world. As Middleton puts it, "the human vocation is modelled on the nature and actions of the God portrayed in Genesis 1."[241]

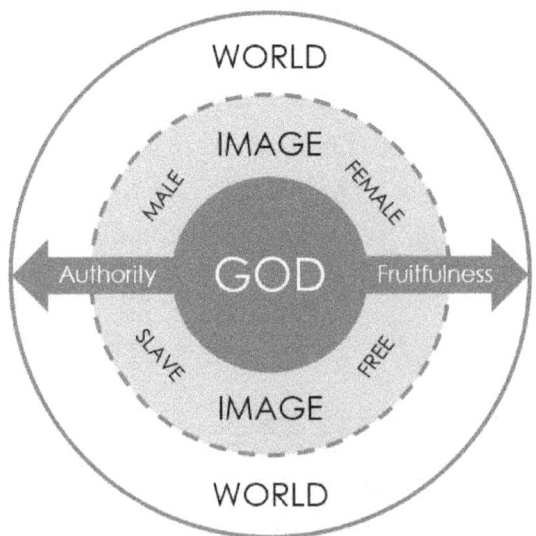

Fig. K – The Image of God in Creation

---

[241] Middleton, *The Liberating Image*, 60.

Image and Creation

If we take these four hallmarks of image identity in Genesis 1:26-28 and compare them up with Paul's description of Christ as the image of God (Col 1:15-20), we find that there is a striking comparison to be made. Following the chiasmus in from the edge, the claims concerning Christ follow the same sequence of Genesis 1. As God's image (Col 1:15a cf. Gen 1:27), Christ carries the "fullness" of God's presence (Col 1:19 cf. *tselem*, צֶלֶם Gen 1:26); as such, he bears God's life-giving power (Col 1:15b, 18 cf. "be fruitful and multiply and fill the earth", Gen 1:28), and exercises God's authority over all creation and the church (Col 1:16, 18 cf. "fill the earth and subdue it", Gen 1:28).

The only aspect that does not explicitly feature is unity, although this may be identified in Paul's description of all things created and held together "in him" (Col 1:16, 17). It would be all too easy to lose sight of Christ's divinity in pursuit of this correlation, but as we have already attested, Paul's advanced Christology asserts both the supremacy of Christ's divinity and the perfection of his humanity. Nevertheless, his confirmation as the prototype for true humanity runs alongside the exaltation of his divine agency, and it is on the basis of both that his pre-eminence is proclaimed."[242]

---

[242] Cf. Martin, *Colossians and Philemon*, 108; Beetham, *Echoes of Scripture*, 242.

Chapter Ten
HUMANITY, THE IMAGE

Paul's second mention of εἰκών in Colossians (Col 3:10) completes his anthropological narrative. Having established Christ's divinity, sovereignty and perfect humanity through his identification as the image of God, Paul reserves perhaps his most astonishing claim for the Colossians themselves: as they know Christ (Col 2:2), live in him (2:6), die with him (2:12a, 20) and rise with him (2:12b; 3:1), they too are in the process of being renewed into this same image (cf. 2 Cor 4:16; Rom 12:2). There is disagreement about whether κτίσαντος (ktisantos, "creator") here refers to God,[243] or to Christ,[244] but the implication for humanity is the same. Paul's Christological claim is, after all, that Jesus is simultaneously God and His image.[245]

---

[243] As per Martin, *Colossians and Philemon*, 107; O'Brien, *Colossians, Philemon*, 191; Sumney, *Writing "In the Image" of Scripture*, 211.
[244] As per Fee, *Pauline Christology*, 304; Moo, *Colossians and Philemon*, 270; Thompson, *Colossians and Philemon*, 78.
[245] O'Brien, *Colossians, Philemon*, 191.

The Colossian Image

This time there is no question among interpreters that Paul is alluding to Genesis 1:26-27 to make a typological statement.[246] It is also broadly agreed that this passage connects directly to Colossians 1:15, not only because of the repetition of εἰκών, but also because of the corresponding emphasis on redemption that surrounds each reference.[247]

In which case, there are two important implications we must address. Firstly, that everything in between 1:15 and 3:10 is about moving the Colossians from accepting the image of God as an identity for Christ, to one they can also grow into. Secondly, that we should understand the image in 3:10 as bearing the same hallmarks as the image in 1:15. This could imply a process of divinization, in which our 'eikonic' status reflects the divinity of Christ. However, that is not the essential effect of εἰκών here. Rather, it is the realignment of humanity with the foundations of its creation, such that it bears once more the full blessing of its sinless, righteous, pre-Fall identity.

---

[246] Dunn, *Colossians and Philemon*, 222; Martin, *Colossians and Philemon*, 107; Beetham, *Echoes of Scripture*, 241, 244; Sumney, *Writing "In the Image" of Scripture*, 210-11; O'Brien, *Colossians, Philemon*, 191; Fee, *Pauline Christology*, 303; Thompson, *Colossians and Philemon*, 78; Moo, *Colossians and Philemon*, 269.
[247] E.g. Wright, *Colossians and Philemon*, 143; Thompson, *Colossians and Philemon*, 78; Beetham, *Echoes of Scripture*, 242.

Humanity, the Image

Yet, in the wake of Adam's transgression (Rom 5:14), Christ has overcome the sting of death by taking Adam's place as the prototype human (Rom 5:12-21; 1 Cor 15:45-49), radically redefining what it means to carry those blessings. No longer are the hallmarks of humanity confined by the limitations of mortal earthly parameters, now they are unleashed to the fullest potential of the one who is pre-eminent in creation, whose humanity is lived out in the heavenly realms.

In Romans, Paul outlines what this entails: justification, which restores communion with God in Christ (Rom 5:16, 21); dominion (Rom 5:17, 21); and life (Rom 5:18, 21). The very hallmarks we have attributed to the image of God. In Colossians, Paul builds the same Adam Christology through the connection to 1:15.[248] *That* is the image into which we are renewed.

It is significant that Paul describes this 'eikonic' renewal as the difference between the old ἄνθρωπον (anthropon, 3:9)[249] and the new (3:10).[250] Often translated as "self" (e.g., NRSV, ESV, NIV), a better rendering would be "humanity," as indeed the NRSV and NIV do translate it

---

[248] On this, see Martin, *Colossians and Philemon*, 107; Dunn, *Colossians and Philemon*, 221-22; O'Brien, *Colossians, Philemon*, 190-91; Wall, *Colossians and Philemon*, 142.
[249] Cf. "the body of the flesh," Colossians 2:11; cf. Romans 6:6.
[250] Cf. Ephesians 4:22-24.

in Ephesians 2:15.²⁵¹ The KJV probably stands as the best mainstream translation here, giving "man" for ἄνθρωπον, whereas the NLT's "sinful nature" is not allowed for by the text, even if it is a good interpretation of the intention of the text.

Important disagreements on this point have been offered by Gordon Fee, who interprets Colossians 3:9-10 as describing an inner, ethical renewal rather than a process of recreation, and James Dunn, who argues that Paul is describing a new way of living.²⁵² In each case, their arguments must be granted, but I believe they underestimate the extent of the restoration God intends for humanity. What Paul envisions is nothing short of a total reconfiguration of humanity, back to its original calling, yet exalted even more so in its participation with the risen Christ.²⁵³ Paul's use of baptismal imagery here, indicated by the movement from an old self that is ἀπεκδυσάμενοι (apekdysamenoi, "stripped off," Col 3:9) and a new self which must be ἐνδυσάμενοι (endysamenoi, "clothed," Col 3:10), which is widely acknowledged to be evoking the baptismal setting of the early church, if not

---

²⁵¹ This is similarly affirmed by O'Brien, *Colossians, Philemon*, 190; Thompson, *Colossians and Philemon*, 77-78; and Wall, *Colossians and Philemon*, 142.
²⁵² Fee, *Pauline Christology*, 304; Dunn, *Colossians and Philemon*, 221.
²⁵³ Cf. Wright, *Colossians and Philemon*, 143.

Humanity, the Image

quoting baptismal liturgy, powerfully underpins this picture of transformation.[254]

At the heart of this is the promise of God's indwelling Spirit. Colossians has been criticised for its lack of pneumatology,[255] but that does not mean Paul undervalues the participation of and with the Spirit. In fact, the Spirit is mentioned directly (Col 1:8), and implied often (Col 1:9, 11, 19; 2:5, 9), but the emphasis throughout Colossians is the importance of Christ, since it is his sovereignty, divinity and humanity that seems to have been cast in shadow in the Colossian church. Nevertheless, Paul's identification of Christ as the image of God artfully includes the Spirit as it is through the Spirit that an "emptied" Jesus (Phil 2:7) experienced the promised indwelling of the image of God (Col 1:19; 2:9; cf. Mt 3:16; Mk 1:10; Lk 3:22, note ref. to "bodily"; Jn 1:32-33). The fact that this whole letter, and the two references to the image in particular, are steeped in baptismal language and liturgy only serves to make this point all the stronger. In this sense, wherever Christ is named, the Spirit by association goes with him.

---

[254] Wright, *Colossians and Philemon*, 138-39; Fee, *Pauline Christology*, 303; Sumney, *Writing "In the Image" of Scripture*, 212; Moo, *Colossians and Philemon*, 266; cf. Dunn, *Colossians and Philemon*, 221.
[255] Lincoln, *Colossians*, 570; Dunn, *Colossians and Philemon*, 221; cf. Fee, *Pauline Christology*, 647.

The Colossian Image

The same is true of the renewed image of God in Colossians 3:10. Through the indwelling of the Spirit the presence of God fills the renewed, true humanity so that the sovereignty and life-giving power of God is released to the world through His image.[256] And it really is *to the world*, not only Israel. Paul's depiction of renewed humanity (Col 3:11; cf. Gal 3:28), which Wall calls Paul's "Magna Carta,"[257] is in the form of a reunification,[258] to God and one another:

> In that renewal there is no longer Greek and Jew, circumcised and uncircumcised, barbarian, Scythian, slave and free; but Christ is all and in all!
> Colossians 3:11

Notably, Paul has introduced a shift from unity portrayed in terms of gender (Gen 1:27) to caste (Col 3:11 cf. 1 Cor 12:3). Far from rejecting the original pattern, however, Paul simply applies it to his own world. We have already recognised in chapter nine that the image of God was a democratising force within humanity, not a privileged status reserved for the elite but a part of the innermost being of all peoples of the earth. However,

---

[256] Cf. Moo, *Colossians and Philemon*, 268.
[257] Wall, *Colossians and Philemon*, 144.
[258] Barclay, *Colossians and Philemon*, 79.

Humanity, the Image

whereas humanity in Genesis 1 had only one distinction to unify, that of gender, the humanity of Paul's day was fragmented across so many social and religious frontiers that the reunification needed was on a grander scale. Specifically, Paul identifies those elements of race, religion, and class that separate a person from God's chosen people, and declares every barrier removed.[259] Thus the humanity that is being restored truly reflects the equality and unity that was a key component of its original creation (Gen 1:27).

This sharing of divine communion, authority and life is a feature of the true human experience. Rather than speaking of divinization, then, we might better view the effect of Paul's 'advanced Christology' as drawing up with it a 'high anthropology', akin to a form of anthropological theosis, in which humans remain human yet become Christ-like, therefore like God, as they experience the divine moving through them.

This is fundamentally a missionary calling, since it envisions the continued expansion of God's Kingdom through the advancement of His image, and so as well as bearing the hallmarks of the Image of God in creation,

---

[259] Others to argue similarly include Lincoln, *Colossians*, 570-71; O'Brien, *Colossians, Philemon*, 191-92; Wright, *Colossians and Philemon*, 144; Beetham, *Echoes of Scripture*, 241; Dunn, *Colossians and Philemon*, 223; Moo, *Colossians and Philemon*, 270-71; Thompson, *Colossians and Philemon*, 79.

The Colossian Image

humanity must also serve as Christ's witness (Acts 1:8) by walking in the ways of the image of Wisdom, and by proclaiming the Lordship of the image against Empire. This is achieved, says Paul, by living "in Christ" (Col 2:6).[260] Therefore, in Part Three, we shall consider how Paul expects this 'eikonic' vision for humanity to be put into practice.

---

[260] Fee, *Pauline Christology*, 303.

PART THREE

Life 'in Christ' in Colossians

As you therefore have received Christ Jesus the Lord,
continue to live your lives in him.

Colossians 2:6

Chapter Eleven

LIVING 'IN HIM'

If the most celebrated aspect of Colossians is Paul's exalted portrayal of Christ,[261] then the most contested is his rendering of life in Christ that dominates the remainder of the letter. Typically the debate has gravitated towards the nature of Paul's complaint against the Colossians, which impresses itself as an ominous companion to Paul's vision for life "in him" (Col 2:8-23). Indeed, many have argued that the complaint is the primary motivation for the epistle.[262] However, it is important not to lose sight of Paul's overarching intent. The relatively gentle tone of the letter as a whole, in comparison with Galatians for example, suggests that

---

[261] Most notably in Colossians 1:13-23, but also clearly evident in Colossians 1:27; 2:2-3, 9-10, 15; 3:1, 3.

[262] E.g. Bornkamm, "The Heresy of Colossians," in *Conflict at Colossae: A Problem in the Interpretation of Early Christianity Illustrated by Selected Modern Studies* 123; Arnold, *The Colossian Syncretism*, 6; Moo, *Colossians and Philemon*, 47; Dunn, *Colossians and Philemon*, 23; Barth and Blanke, *Colossians*, 44.

while there clearly is a problem, it is not Paul's leading concern.[263] Rather, he offers a bigger vision for life 'in Christ'; one that incorporates the threats within the community to show how they may be overcome and describes the transformed life the Colossians have commenced.

Nevertheless, an appraisal of the problem is necessary, not because it is the major issue at play, but because Paul raises it as the entry point into seeing the full implications of life 'in Christ'. Such a complex and disputed issue will take some careful unpacking, but will give us a more complete picture of the premise for Paul's vision of a transformed Christian life.

The question is, how does Paul's presentation of life 'in Christ' relate to his understanding of true humanity? In answering this, I hope to show that Paul is offering not only a practical manual of 'warning' and 'teaching' (Col 1:28) for how to reflect the true humanity of Christ, but a remarkable insight into the process of transformation, in which we are incorporated into Christ as we participate with him, thereby assuming our true humanity as the renewed image of God (3:10).

---

[263] Cf. Hooker, "Were There False Teachers in Colossae?," in *Christ and Spirit in the New Testament: Studies in Honour of Charles Francis Digby Moule* 316.

Living 'In Him'

The "in him" framework

The frequency of the phrases "in Christ," "in him" (referring to Christ) and "in me" (in the case of Jesus speaking about himself) throughout the New Testament,[264] most especially in the Pauline corpus,[265] suggest this was a familiar concept in the early church. Several of Paul's letters begin by classifying those he is writing to as "in Christ" (1 Cor 1:2, 30; Eph 1:1; Phil 1:1; Col 1:2; 2 Tim 1:1). Individual Christians are also spoken of in the same way (Rom 16:3, 7, 9, 10; 1 Cor 4:17; 2 Cor 12:2; Phil 4:21; Phm 23).

On one level, this can refer to a person's or community's association with Christ (Rom 4:5; 9:33; 10:11, 14; Gal 2:16; Eph 1:13; 3:12; Phil 1:26, 29; 3:3, 9; Col 1:4; 1 Tim 1:16; 2 Tim 3:15). However, its prevailing function within the Pauline

---

[264] Mt 14:2; Mk 6:14; Lk 22:17; 23:22; Jn 1:4; 6:56; 10:30; 11:26; 13:31, 32; 14:10, 11, 20; 15:2, 4, 5, 6, 7; 16:33; 17:21, 23; Acts 17:28; Heb 3:14; 1 Pet 3:16; 5:10, 14; 1 Jn 1:5; 2:4, 5, 6, 8, 10, 15, 27, 28; 3:5, 6, 15, 17, 24; 4:13, 15, 16; 5:20. These do not count uses that refer to faith or belief "in Christ/him/me."

[265] Again, not including references to faith "in Christ/him," the phrase "in Christ" is used 79 times in the Pauline corpus. Colossians uses this phrase four times (Col 1:2, 4, 28; 2:5), paling to the 27 uses in Romans. "In him," with reference to Christ, is used 23 times. It is notable for this study that the most frequent use of "in him" is to be found in Colossians, with eight uses: Col 1:17, 19; 2:6, 7, 9, 10, 11, 15.

corpus is to encapsulate something far greater. That is, the all-encompassing fullness of the Christian life.

Christians are chosen in Christ (Eph 1:4, 11),[266] justified, sanctified and redeemed in Christ (Rom 3:24; 1 Cor 1:2; Gal 2:16-17; 3:14; Eph 1:7; Phil 3:9; cf. 2 Cor 5:19; 2 Tim 2:10), righteous in Christ (Rom 4:5, 24; 2 Cor 5:21; Phil 3:9), triumphant in Christ (2 Cor 2:14; Col 2:15), adopted in Christ (Gal 3:26). They are a new creation in Christ (2 Cor 5:17; cf. Eph 2:10), blessed in Christ (Eph 1:3; Phil 4:19), recipients of grace and mercy (1 Cor 1:4; 1 Tim 1:16; 2 Tim 1:9; 2:1), hope (Rom 15:12) and eternal life (Rom 6:23; Phil 3:14) in Christ. They are set free from sin and death in Christ (Rom 8:1-2; cf. Gal 2:4; Eph 2:13), yet they have also died in Christ (1 Cor 15:18). They are connected to the love of God in Christ (Rom 8:39; 1 Tim 1:14; 2 Tim 1:13), and to one another in Christ (2 Cor 1:21; Eph 1:10; 2:22; Col 1:17). They are truthful in Christ (Rom 9:1; 2 Cor 2:17), wise in Christ (1 Cor 4:10; cf. 1 Cor 1:5), and they are one body in Christ (Rom 12:5; cf. Eph 3:6). They may be infants in Christ (1 Cor 3:1) or mature in Christ (Col 1:28). But in all things, they live and are made alive in Christ (Rom 6:11, 23; 1 Cor 15:22; Eph 2:5-7).

---

[266] Cf. Romans 8:29, another "predestination" passage which does not speak of being "in Christ/him" but does use "image of God" language to communicate a similar message. The connection to Jewish ideas of election are clearly in the foreground here.

Living 'In Him'

This theme is introduced in Colossians through the use of ἐν Χριστῷ (en christo, "in Christ"), which features at key scene-setting points in the letter. Just as the Colossians *are* in Christ (Col 1:2 cf. 1:4), Paul's hope is to see them *mature* in Christ (1:28 cf. 2:5). Thus we glimpse Paul's inaugurated eschatology, in which the heavenly identity they already bear may be drawn ever more from their future promised experience into their present reality.[267] However, life in Christ finds its fullest expression in the repeated phrases ἐν αὐτῷ (en auto, "in him," Col 1:16, 17, 19; 2:6, 7, 9, 10) and ἐν ω (en o, "in whom," Col 2:3, 11, 12).

These references are grouped into two passages (1:15-20 and 2:6-19) which hold the whole letter together and unveil a narrative thread to Paul's Christology and anthropology: God's presence, authority, and life are found in Christ (1:15-17; 2:9, 15), and if humanity lives 'in him', it will share these blessings (1:18-20; 2:6-7, 10-14). In each case, the 'in him' theme is used as the framework on which this narrative hangs.

Typically, any study of life in Christ in Colossians will zero in on the passage identified as discussing a deception in Colossae (2:6-23), and it is easy to see why. Whereas in Colossians 1:15-20 the emphasis of "in him" is clearly on Christ's identity, in 2:6-23 the emphasis shifts to construct a theological and practical vision for the life of the

---

[267] Dunn, *Colossians and Philemon*, 36; Wall, *Colossians and Philemon*, 18; O'Brien, *Colossians, Philemon*, xlvi.

The Colossian Image

Church.[268] However, it is important that we do not jump to the conclusion before paying attention to the foundation.

The vision of Christian life "in him," as opposed to whatever problem existed among the Colossians, finds its roots in the Christ hymn. This may be demonstrated by a comparison of the units, which finds several credentials associated with Christ in Colossians 1:15-20 that are relocated to the Church in Colossians 2:6-19. In him, the Church receives fullness (Col 2:10; cf. Col 1:19; 2:9), authority over rulers and powers (Col 2:10; cf. Col 1:16; 2:15), resurrection (Col 2:12; cf. Col 1:18), and peace made on the cross (Col 2:14; cf. Col 1:20). Before we examine life 'in him' as set against the 'heresy', therefore, we must first see how Paul lays the foundations of life 'in him' in the Christ hymn.

He does this by highlighting to his readers what is found 'in Christ' when they live 'in him'. While the chiastic structure of Colossians 1:15-20 highlights both the divinity and prototypical humanity of Christ, if we isolate the three ἐν αὐτῷ statements we find more than revelations about Christ; we find indicators of humanity's place within creation as a result of Christ's agency. In Christ, humanity was created (1:16), and so only with Christ can

---

[268] Note the use of the plural ὑμᾶς (humas, "you," Col 2:8, 13, 16, 18), indicating that it is the Colossian Church, and not individual Christians that Paul is addressing.

Living 'In Him'

humans truly rediscover their being, and with it their potential. In Christ humanity was held together with the whole of creation (1:17), and so only with Christ can humans rediscover their place within creation, and with it their purpose. Finally, on the basis of God dwelling in Christ (1:19), humanity has now been reconciled once more (1:20), and so only with Christ can anyone rediscover the peace and prominence God intends for their lives.

This 'in him' framework takes Paul's readers into the history and scope of humanity's relationship with God, from creation to redemption, from earth to heaven, as it places Christ at the centre of all things. What is astonishing is that Paul uses this same 'in him' framework to indicate that the blessings located in Christ are now accessible to his Church. Having established what is found "in him," Paul invites the Colossians to "continue your lives *in him*, rooted and built up *in him*" (2:6-7). This is surely more than an instruction to live according to the teachings of Christ. It is an invitation for the Colossians to rediscover and fulfil their potential, their purpose, and their prominence in creation through their relationship with Christ.

What follows in the body of the letter is a commission to live according to this invitation, guarding against the stumbling blocks that will prevent a wholehearted entrance into this new life with Christ, and highlighting the fruit to expect when they do enter. At the heart of this fruit is the promise of total renewal, as they "strip off the old humanity, with its associated deeds, and put on the new" (Col 3:9-10, translation mine). The question, then, is what does this new life look like? Paul's first answer is first to assert what it is not.

Chapter Twelve

THE COLOSSIAN DECEPTION

As mentioned above, the majority of the ἐν αὐτῷ / ἐν ᾧ (en auto/en o, "in him"/"in whom") references are to be found in Colossians 2:6-23, which is widely regarded as a unit in which Paul confronts problems within the Colossian Church. These problems, which cover issues surrounding spiritual allegiance (Col 2:8, 18), attitude (Col 2:18), and behaviour (Col 2:16, 18), stand in opposition to living 'in Christ' (Col 2:6), in whom the Colossians are rooted and built up (Col 2:7), in whom dwells the fullness of God (Col 2:9), in whom they attain fullness (Col 2:10), in whom they are circumcised spiritually (Col 2:11), and with whom they are buried and raised to new life (Col 2:12; 3:10). Paul's point is clear enough: The truth is only to be found in the gospel (Col 1:5), as expressed in the death and resurrection of Christ (Col 1:20; 2:12). Any alternative is but a deception (cf. κενῆς ἀπάτης, "empty deceit," Col 2:8).

The Colossian Image

Attempts to define this deception have consumed years of scholarly effort but have yet to approach a consensus.[269] The common tendency has been to assume there must have been one specific problem Paul was confronting, clear to his original readers, but obscured by the deteriorating effects of time and distance, so that all we have left is a collection of perplexing clues.[270] The task, then, becomes a complex dot-to-dot puzzle, in which each clue represents a dot without number.[271] If only we knew the context well enough then we would be able to place the clues in the right order and join the dots to reveal the original picture.[272]

---

[269] O'Brien, Barclay and Moo all include helpful summaries of the scholarship thus far on this complex issue in their commentaries. Between them they cover the most influential arguments (those of Lightfoot, Dibelius, Bornkamm, Francis, Schweizer, Dunn, Hooker, and Arnold). Most interpreters will fall broadly within one of these. O'Brien, *Colossians, Philemon*, xxx-xxxviii; Barclay, *Colossians and Philemon*, 39-48; Moo, *Colossians and Philemon*, 46-60.
[270] Arnold, *The Colossian Syncretism*, 5-6; Lightfoot, "The Colossian Heresy," in *Conflict at Colossae: A Problem in the Interpretation of Early Christianity Illustrated by Selected Modern Studies* 14; Martin, *Colossians and Philemon*, 8; Bornkamm, *The Heresy of Colossians*, 123.
[271] Barclay argues similarly, but using the metaphor of a jigsaw puzzle: Barclay, *Colossians and Philemon*, 51-52.
[272] Cf. Stettler, "The Opponents at Colossae," in *Paul and his Opponents* 173.

The Colossian Deception

Among the first serious attempts at this came from J. B. Lightfoot. His detection of Jewish language (Sabbath, festivals, special food, circumcision: Col 2:16; 2:11, 13), combined with a "theosophic speculation" that pursued a "shadowy mysticism" (cf. Col 1:26, 27; 2:2; 4:3) through an ascetic lifestyle (Col 2:18, 23), led him to identify a form of Jewish Gnosticism.[273] Gunther Bornkamm developed this idea by identifying Oriental Aeon-theology interwoven into Diaspora Judaism, to diagnose a Jewish Gnosticism infused with Hellenistic syncretism.[274] This appeared neatly to join all of the dots, and remained influential for many years.[275] However, subsequent studies have suggested a later, second-century emergence of Gnosticism,[276] with what Clinton Arnold described as "substantive differences of thought when compared to the teaching of the Colossian opponents."[277]

That is not to say that there is no insight to glean. Of particular value is the importance given to the extensive

---

[273] Specifically, he argued for a connection with Essenism. Even while the link to gnostic thought has been largely dismissed, the connection to the Essenes has remained in view, especially in light of the subsequent discoveries at Qumran. Lightfoot, *The Colossian Heresy*, 13-37; cf. Barclay, *Colossians and Philemon*, 40-42; Bruce, "The Colossian Heresy," *Bibliotheca Sacra* 200.
[274] Bornkamm, *The Heresy of Colossians*, 125-137.
[275] Indeed, it still is in some areas of scholarship, especially Germany: Barclay, *Colossians and Philemon*, 42.
[276] Moo, *Colossians and Philemon*, 53.
[277] Arnold, *The Colossian Syncretism*, 1.

use of Jewish language. While attempts have been made to explain the deception in terms of an entirely pagan influence (see Tables A and B), in the end, the reliance not only of Colossians 2:6-23 but of the letter as a whole on words, concepts and references drawn from the Old Testament cannot be dismissed.[278]

Much of this we have already seen in the previous chapters of this study, and to this we might add the obvious significance of circumcision (Col 2:11, 13 cf. Gen 17:9-10), an oblique reference to the Law (Col 2:14), which is then extrapolated into regulations concerning food and drink (Col 2:16 cf. Lev 11:1-23; Deut 14:3-21; Dan 1:8), the Jewish rhythms of "festivals, new moons, and Sabbaths" (Col 2:16 cf. Ex 23:10-19; 1 Chr 23:31; Neh 10:33; Hos 2:11; Eze 45:17), the mediation of angels (Col 2:18 cf. Ex 23:21) and regulations governing cleanliness (Col 2:21; cf. Lev 11:24-45; Num 5:1-4; 19:11).

That is not to say that these traces of paganism or Hellenism should be discounted altogether. It may be argued that the best attempts to join the most dots and give some idea of the original picture are those that allow

---

[278] In addition to these references, Marianne Meye Thompson makes several connections to the beliefs circulating in first-century Christianity and Judaism, including attraction to asceticism, angels, and mysteries: Thompson, *Colossians and Philemon*, 7-8. Cf. for asceticism: *LAris* 142; for angels: 3 En 12:5; Philo, *De somnis* 1.141-43, Justin Martyr, *Dialogue* 34.2; for mysteries: Apuleius, *Metamorphoses*.

The Colossian Deception

for some form of Jewish syncretistic influence alive in the Colossian Church, be that a Hellenised ascetic mysticism, as Fred Francis has claimed,[279] or a Phrygian folk-magic religion, as per Clinton Arnold.[280] Although these interpretations draw on different understandings for some of the key features of the deception, most notably θρησκεία τῶν ἀγγέλων (threskeia ton aggelon, "worship of angels," Col 2:18),[281] and neither are without their problems,[282] they do both seek to hold in tension the indications of both Jewish and Gentile concepts, and in so

---

[279] Francis, "Humility and Angelic Worship in Col 2:18," in *Conflict at Colossae: A Problem in the Interpretation of Early Christianity Illustrated by Selected Modern Studies* 166; See also O'Brien, *Colossians, Philemon*, xxxvii-xxxviii; Bruce, *The Colossian Heresy*, 200.

[280] Arnold, *The Colossian Syncretism*, 310-12.

[281] Both Francis and Arnold see this reference to be central to understanding the deception in Colossae, but their differing interpretations of the genitive "of angels" leads them in very different directions. Put briefly, Francis argued that this was a subjective genitive, indicating a deception founded on joining in with the worship the angels offer to God. Arnold, on the other hand, insists that it must be taken as an objective genitive, indicating worshipping the angels themselves. Francis, *Humility and Angelic Worship in Col 2:18*, 176-81; Arnold, *The Colossian Syncretism*, 8-10, 90-95.

[282] E.g. Francis does not explain why Paul needs to make a point of elevating Christ in this scheme: Moo, *Colossians and Philemon*, 55. Whereas Arnold's case is drawn too heavily from later texts, without sufficient first-century evidence: Moo, *Colossians and Philemon*, 58-59.

Table A – Potential Gnostic and Mystic Influences

PROPONENT	PROPOSAL	FOR	AGAINST
J.B. LIGHTFOOT	Jewish Gnosticism	- Recognition of Jewish language - Potential link with Essenism	- Reliance on Gnosticism
GUNTHER BORNKAMM	Hellenistic Syncretism	- Recognition of Jewish language - Connects στοιχεῖα (Col 2:8) to Oriental Aeon-theology	- Reliance on Gnosticism
MARTIN DIBELIUS[283]	Pagan Mysticism	- Connects στοιχεῖα (Col 2:8) and ἐμβατεύω (Col 2:18) with pagan cultic initiation rites	- No account for Jewish language - Too much weight placed on the meaning of one word
FRED O. FRANCIS	Jewish Mysticism	- Recognition of Jewish language - Deduces worship 'with' angels, not 'of' angels in Col 2:18	- Too much reliance on interpretation of angel worship - No account of why Paul would criticise this

---

[283] In particular, he finds its use in the initiation rites of the cult of Apollo: Dibelius, "The Isis Initiation," in *Conflict at Colossae: A Problem in the Interpretation of Early Christianity Illustrated by Selected Modern Studies* 83-90.

Table B – Potential Hellenistic Influences

PROPONENT	PROPOSAL	FOR	AGAINST
EDUARD SCHWEIZER[284]	Pythagorean Philosophy	- Connects στοιχεῖα (Col 2:8), food laws and ascetism to neo-Pythagoreanism	- Too little account of Jewish language - Lack of evidence for philosophical syncretism in rural Phrygia[285]
R.E. DEMARIS[286]	Middle-Platonic Philosophy	- Connects Col 2:20-23 to Middle-Platonic demonology - Views it as Jewish syncretism	- Lack of evidence for philosophical syncretism in rural Phrygia
TROY MARTIN[287]	Cynic Philosophy	- Connects references to ascetism and abstinence to Cynicism	- Lack of evidence for philosophical syncretism in rural Phrygia

---

[284] Schweizer, *Colossians*, 125-33.
[285] Arnold, *The Colossian Syncretism*, 3.
[286] DeMaris, *The Colossian Controversy*, vol. 96.
[287] Martin, *By Philosophy and Empty Deceit*, 104.

doing are able to rationalise the practice of early Christianity within a highly syncretistic first-century Near-Eastern world.[288]

If Paul is confronting a deception with a significant Jewish dimension, to which the Colossian Christians are vulnerable, and especially if that deception is syncretistic in nature, then it is notable that the juxtaposition of warnings and 'in him' assurances counter the idea that anything except Christ is necessary for initiation into the kingdom (Col 2:11-13), or to attain fullness (2:10). All other authorities, spiritual, political, cosmic and earthly, are subject to Christ (1:15-16; 2:10, 15).

Thus, the danger becomes one of idolatry, in which "all other lords become idols when contrasted with Christ."[289] While our focus is on the syncretistic element, such idols appear to draw from pagan influences. Angels, astral powers, the desire for mystery, all become channels to God.[290] In reply Paul asserts that Christ alone has cosmic authority (1:15-16; 2:9-10, 15), Christ is the only mystery (1:27; 2:2), Christ the only channel to the presence, wisdom and knowledge of God (1:9; 2:9-10; 3:16).

Alternatively, if we switch our focus to the Jewish element, then it might imply that the most immediate idol standing in opposition to Christ is the Law. Not only does

---

[288] Cf. Thompson, *Colossians and Philemon*, 62.
[289] Wright, *Colossians and Philemon*, 108.
[290] Cf. Martin, *Colossians and Philemon*, 95.

Paul scrutinise rituals that are closely associated with the Torah (2:11, 16, 20b-22),[291] but evocative terminology such as στοιχεῖα (stoicheira, "elemental spirits/principles," Col 2:8, 20),[292] χειρόγραφον and δόγμασιν (cheirographon and dogmasin, "record" and "legal demands," Col 2:14) could also be understood as references to the Law.[293] If so, the Law is denounced as "not according to Christ" (2:8) and is dismissed (2:14 cf. Rom 10:4; Gal 3:10-14, 23-26) as a mere "shadow" of Christ (2:17).[294] However, there are a number of problems with this view.

Firstly, it is important to note that the term "law" (νόμος, nomos) does not feature in this passage, or at all in Colossians. Secondly, while the specific symptoms Paul names can be identified as important aspects of Jewish life

---

[291] Thompson, *Colossians and Philemon*, 62; Dunn, *Colossians and Philemon*, 171. Some have argued that the reference to angel worship points to the same conclusion, if Paul's objection was to venerating the angels as bearers of the Law (Ex 23:21; cf. Acts 7:53; Gal 3:19).

[292] Herold Weiss argues that this can be translated as "principles" and is a reference to the Torah. Weiss, "The Law in the Epistle to the Colossians," *Catholic Biblical Quarterly* 294.

[293] Bandstra, *The Law and the Elements of the World*, 159-60; Bruce, "Christ as Conqueror and Reconciler," *Bibliotheca Sacra* 295.

[294] As per Johnson, "The Paralysis of Legalism" *Bibliotheca Sacra* ; Kim, *Paul and the New Perspective* ; Westerholm, *Perspectives Old and New in Paul*.

in the Old Testament, they are not all, strictly speaking, to be found in the Torah. There are no drink laws,[295] nor any tripartite configuration of festivals, new moons and Sabbaths, which is a later development (1 Chr 23:31; 2 Chr 2:4; 8:13; 31:3; Neh 10:33; Hos 2:11; Eze 45:17).[296] Thirdly, it is inconsistent with Jesus' own proclamation that he came to fulfil and not abolish the law (Mt 5:17), which is in keeping with Paul's theology (Rom 3:31; 6:15; 7:12) and determination to keep the Law himself (Acts 18, 24:14, 25:8; Rom 7:22).

Perhaps, then, Paul's criticism is not with the Law, per se, but with a legalistic approach to it.[297] However, in light of E. P. Sanders' research, it is clear that first-century Palestinian Judaism was not the legalistic religion it has so often been stereotyped to be.[298] And if Dunn is correct that there is little evidence for significant distinctions

---

[295] Dunn points to restraint developing among "scrupulous Jews" in later years, especially in the Diaspora where there was increased risk of consuming drink offered in libations (cf. Dan 1:3-16; 10:3; cf. Rom 14:21), but no law governing such attitudes: Dunn, *Colossians and Philemon*, 173; cf. Stettler, *The Opponents at Colossae*, 180.

[296] Each is named independently in the Torah, but it seems clear that it is the later Old Testament use of the three together that is in view here.

[297] O'Brien, *Colossians, Philemon*, xxxix; Wall, *Colossians and Philemon*, 120-22; Weiss, *The Law in the Epistle to the Colossians*, 312.

[298] Sanders, *Paul and Palestinian Judaism*.

between Palestinian and Diaspora Judaism, then it seems unlikely that Paul would perceive a legalistic approach to the Law to be a pressing danger.[299] Nevertheless, it is clear that Paul's use of distinctly Jewish language is deliberate and significant, and that it challenges the traditional Jewish understanding of how to walk with God.[300] How, then, are we to understand this challenge? We will consider this in the next chapter.

---

[299] Dunn, *Colossians and Philemon*, 30.
[300] The language of walking is pertinent here, given the Old Testament instruction to "walk in the way that the Lord your God has commanded you" (Deut 5:33) and Paul's command "walk in him" (περιπατεῖτε ἐν αὐτῷ, peripateite en auto, Col 2:6) at the start of this unit.

Chapter Thirteen

RELOCATING LAW INTO CHRIST

We must begin by challenging some of the underlying assumptions. For all the "bewildering variety of scholarly reconstructions"[301] regarding the Colossian deception, where they coalesce is in their assumption that there is only one way to join the dots, only one picture to be discovered. This assumption has been challenged by Morna Hooker, who suggests that Paul may actually be offering warnings against a range of potential deceptions that surround the church.[302]

There is much to like about this. For one thing, if Paul's intent is to highlight potential threats rather than contend with one already raging, it explains why his tone is gentler here than in his confrontations of the problems in Galatia and Corinth. Indeed, Paul's opening assertion that the Colossians *are* "holy and faithful brothers in Christ" (Col

---

[301] Moo, *Colossians and Philemon*, 47.
[302] Hooker, *Were There False Teachers in Colossae?* 317-18.

1:2), sets a context in which preserving that faithfulness seems more fitting than denying it. Hooker also points to Paul's exhortation of the Colossians' faith (Col 1:4), the fruit of the gospel among them (1:6), their love of the Spirit (1:8), the firmness of their faith (2:5), and the fact that they are rooted and established in faith (2:7) as evidence that the faith of the Colossian Church was not being strangled by an ongoing issue.[303]

For another, it explains how an external threat can be described as though it were an internal problem, which Paul diagnoses is the result of "not holding fast to the head" (Col 2:19).[304] That said, the real value of Hooker's argument is that it draws attention away from the need to discover the specific target of Paul's polemic and toward his reason for making it. Paul's primary intent throughout the letter is not to counter something but to promote someone, "to demonstrate that both creation and redemption are completed in Christ because he has replaced the Jewish law."[305] Therefore, our ability to

---

[303] Hooker, *Were There False Teachers in Colossae?* 318-19.
[304] For internal, see: Barclay, *Colossians and Philemon*, 39; Bornkamm, *The Heresy of Colossians*, 124; Thompson, *Colossians and Philemon*, 53, 54. For external, see: Dunn, *Colossians and Philemon*, 23; Stettler, *The Opponents at Colossae*, 175.
[305] Hooker, *Were The False Teachers in Colossae?* 329; cf. Stettler, *The Opponents at Colossae*, 173-74; Martin, *Colossians and Philemon*, 77-78.

understand Paul's direction of thought, and to see the final picture he is placing before us, is not reliant on us fully comprehending his *Sitz im Leben*, or locating every dot on the page.[306]

Concerns have been raised about Hooker's case, with Douglas Moo highlighting two in particular. Firstly, he argues that the singular nouns φιλοσοφίας (philosophias, "philosophy") and ἀπάτης (apates, "deceit," both Col 2:8) suggest only one deception.[307] Secondly, warnings against being "taken captive" (Col 2:8), "judged" (Col 2:16) or "disqualified" (Col 2:18) imply an external threat.[308] Although the second criticism feels doubtful to me, given the stronger suggestion of an internal threat rooted in "not holding fast to the head" (Col 2:19), the first does need to be addressed.

Even if we accept both, however, these are relatively mild criticisms, and we may find their resolution in the argument of N. T. Wright, who broadly agrees with Hooker.[309] Where he develops the thought is to suggest that each of the problems Paul raises are to be found active within the local Jewish community,[310] indicated by Paul's

---

[306] Contrary to Lincoln, *Colossians*, 561.
[307] Moo, *Colossians and Philemon*, 47-48; cf. Bruce, *The Colossian Heresy*, 195.
[308] Moo, *Colossians and Philemon*, 48; Garland, *Colossians and Philemon*, 141.
[309] Wright, *Paul and the Faithfulness of God*, 992.
[310] Wright, *Paul and the Faithfulness of God*, 992-95.

use of the rare verb συλαγωγῶν (sylagogon, "takes," Col 2:8), which Wright believes to be "a contemptuous pun with the word *synagogue*."[311]

Thus, Wright identifies a mix of over-reliance on Jewish (especially rabbinic) traditions, mixed with a lingering fascination with local deities.[312] This takes us back to a syncretistic view of Phrygian Judaism,[313] except that Wright presses Hooker's point: these elements do not represent an immediate threat to the Christian community, as they did in Galatia, but stand as potential dangers to a faithful, covenantal relationship with Christ.

Taken with James Dunn's assertion that the separation between Jewish and Christian communities had not yet fully taken place,[314] we can then find a way of reconciling a threat that is both multifarious (i.e. syncretistic) yet singular (one Jewish philosophy),[315] both internal (within

---

[311] Wright, *Colossians and Philemon*, 105; cf. Stettler, *The Opponents at Colossae*, 193.
[312] Wright, *Colossians and Philemon*, 26-29, 105-09.
[313] Wright refers to it as paganism rife in the Jewish faith. He does not specify angels, and so this might be seen as a missing dot in his picture, but it is an easy one to fit into this syncretistic view, allowing for either Fred Francis' or Clinton Arnold's picture of Colossian Judaism. Wright, *Paul and the Faithfulness of God*, 993.
[314] Dunn, *Colossians and Philemon*, 29.
[315] Philosophy, for Wright, is not merely a different word for 'religion' (as per Garland), but is a carefully selected frame for his polemic. The Judaism of Colossae has lost so much of its

Relocating Law Into Christ

the wider Jewish/Christian community) and external (outside the Christian faith). When we further add the observation that the Colossian Christians were at least in part, if not predominantly Gentiles (cf. Col 1:12, 27), who had been interwoven into the Christian/Jewish community,[316] we find good reason for Paul to include allusions to the Law in his warning. Not that the Law is inherently bad (as noted above, Romans 7:12 makes the opposite assertion), but that it is fulfilled in Christ and so has no hold over Gentile believers so long as they hold fast to the Head of the body (Col 2:19).[317]

Grace, not Law

Here, then, we confront the second assumption to challenge: namely, that Paul's view of the Law is that it has been replaced by grace as the means for attaining

---

religion, and adopted so much from paganism, that it is a philosophy, not a religion. Wright, *Paul and the Faithfulness of God*, 993; cf. Garland, *Colossians and Philemon*, 141.

[316] Colossians 1:12 – God has enabled them to share in the inheritance; i.e. it is not their inheritance by right. See also Colossians 1:27.

[317] We have already noted in chapter eight Paul's employment of Wisdom theology in correlation with Christ. Wisdom, as the personification of the Law, is now to be identified in the person of Jesus. As such, Christ embodied the Law, and his every word and act is therefore a fulfilment of it. Cf. Thiselton, *The Living Paul*, 46.

righteousness.³¹⁸ Many verses may be taken to point in this direction (e.g., Rom 3:24; 4:16; 6:14; 11:6; Gal 2:21; 5:4; Eph 2:5, 8-9, 13-15) and if correct, surely Paul would feel compelled to confront any mishandling of the Law's role in justification that he perceived in Colossae. Where this idea falls short is in the implication that there was no grace at work in the Law.³¹⁹ As Gordon Wenham asserts, the particular setting for righteousness to be expressed in the Law is within God's covenant with His people:

> Saving history in the Old Testament is built on a series of covenants ... all three covenants are aptly described as acts of divine grace; that is, they are arrangements initiated by God out of his spontaneous mercy, not because of the deserts of those with whom the covenants are made.³²⁰

God's favour was rooted in His unmerited love for Israel. Making this point, Wenham helpfully discusses the correlation between the concept of "favour" in the Old Testament and "grace" in the New Testament. This is emphasised by the frequency with which the LXX

---

³¹⁸ E.g. Bruce, *Christ as Conqueror and Reconciler*, 295-96.
³¹⁹ Achtemeier, *Romans*, 47.
³²⁰ Wenham, "Grace and Law in the Old Testament," in *Law, Morality and the Bible* 3-4.

Relocating Law Into Christ

translates the Hebrew word חֵן (chen, "favour") as χάρις (charis, "grace"). This can be found, for example, in Genesis 6:8; 18:3; 39:21; Exodus 3:21; 11:3; 33:13; Numbers 11:11; 32:5; Deuteronomy 24:1.[321] Love and grace, then, have always shaped God's favour.

Out of this favour flowed covenant (i.e. relationship), and out of covenant flowed Law. Certainly this required obedience (Deut 30:16), but God delighted in it, "because you turn to the Lord with all your heart and all your soul" (Deut 30:10). Indeed, the Sinaitic covenant was established in Exodus 24:7-8 by the covering of blood, before most of the Law had been given and before any of it had been observed![322] Moreover, when we examine the Levitical law codes, we note the prominence given to sacrifices, offerings and cleansing rituals, which operated as the mechanism for the release of God's favour and forgiveness in this covenant relationship.[323]

The pinnacle of this pattern of faith was the Day of Atonement, when all the sins of Israel would be forgiven

---

[321] Wenham, *Grace and Law in the Old Testament*, 4-7.

[322] Note the use of the future tense נַעֲשֶׂה (na'aseh) by Israel in Exodus 24:7: "We *will* do," not "we will *continue* to do."

[323] Of the 613 rules attributed to the Torah, more than one hundred concern the exercise of sacrifices, offerings and cleansing rituals; based on Maimonedes' enumeration, reproduced and discussed in Eisenberg, *The 613 Mitzvot*. We should also note the post-Torah emphasis on God's grace in the Old Testament: e.g., Psalm 86:6; Jeremiah 31:2; Zechariah 12:10.

(Lev 16:1-34) and righteousness restored, by grace, not right living. Thus, grace was fundamental to Israel's relationship with Yahweh, but it was not grace without conditions. For a start, it was grace for Israel. God's favour was reserved for those He had chosen. Even then, it had to be entered into, by repentance and 'works' of sacrifice and ritual.

In this context, it seems most likely that when Paul describes a function of the Law that has been abolished, works of the law that are obsolete in the face of God's *grace*, that he is not dismissing the whole Law, but is showing how the 'works' that identity God's chosen people (circumcision, food laws and festivals; cf. Col 2:11, 16) and confirm the reconciliation of God's people to His side (sacrifices, offerings and cleansing rituals; cf. Col 1:20) have now been fulfilled in Christ on the cross and relocated to him in resurrection. Thus all whose faith is in Christ, Jew and Gentile, may enter into this new covenant (Col 1:12), and participate in Christ's death, which now stands as the one atonement sacrifice that mobilises God's grace, offered to all humanity.

If we take this to be in view in Colossians 2:13-14, as forgiveness and new life result from nailing the record with its legal demands to the cross, especially in light of Paul's assertions in Romans and Galatians that the Law serves to expose sin (Rom 3:20; 7:7; Gal 3:19), then Paul's argument is that although the source of God's grace has

Relocating Law Into Christ

changed, from Law to Christ, the method of receiving it is the same. That is, grace is released by faithful *participation* with the source.

Faith, not legalism

The next assumption we must challenge follows naturally from this: that Paul viewed Judaism as a detrimentally legalistic religion,[324] such that he felt the need to counter legalism wherever he saw it. "By grace you have been saved, though faith ... not the result of works" (Eph 2:8-9) is taken up as the clarion call against every requirement of the Law.

Here again, there are problems. For one thing, it implies that the function of the Law was to save Israel. However, as Gordon Wenham notes, the Sinaitic Law (Ex 20:1-17; Ex 20:22-23:19) was given after Israel's salvation from Egypt had already been assured.[325] In fact, the emphasis of the Law was to *remain* in relationship with Yahweh, not earn one's place at His side. In keeping with this, we find the Torah dominated not by the rules it includes, but by the narrative experience of Israel walking with Yahweh. When Yahweh speaks of Himself, He does so according to relationship: "I am the God of your father, the God of

---

[324] E.g. Johnson, *The Paralysis of Legalism*, 109; Bruce, *The Colossian Heresy*, 197.
[325] Wenham, *Grace and Law in the Old Testament*, 4-6.

Abraham, the God of Isaac, and the God of Jacob" (Ex 3:6). When He gives his commandments, He begins with a relational emphasis: "I am the LORD your God" (Ex 20:2a), which also includes his relational activity: "who brought you out of the land of Egypt, out of the house of slavery" (Ex 20:2b; cf. Deut 5:6; Lev 11:45; 19:36; 25:38; 26:13; Num 15:41; Deut 5:6; Ps 81:10).

It is notable that this is also the way that God identifies Himself when calling His people to heed Him, as opposed to portraying Himself as the God who gave good commandments (e.g. Jos 24:6; Jdg 6:8; 1 Sam 10:18; 2 Kgs 17:36; Jer 11:4; 32:21; Am 2:10; 3:1; Mic 6:4).[326] At every step, the overwhelming preference of the Old Testament is to affirm a faith driven by relationship, not by a legalistic obedience to rules.

A second implication behind the assumption that Paul sought to confront legalism is that he disapproved of a Christian life that continued to adhere to the Torah. Yet Paul expected Christians to "abound in every good work" (2 Cor 9:8), and clearly continued to follow the Law himself (Acts 18:21; 24:14; 25:8). While it may be argued that Paul does this precisely because his freedom from the Law means he is able to say, "To those under the law I became as one under the law" (1 Cor 9:20), that in itself

---

[326] King Jeroboam invokes the same relational identity of Yahweh when he sets up two golden calves in Bethel and Dan: 1 Kgs 12:28.

Relocating Law Into Christ

demonstrates that adherence to the Law cannot be not harmful, and may well be consistent with a faithful expression of Christian life. Taken together, it seems unlikely that Paul was so concerned about the potential for legalism in Colossae that he felt the need to warn against it.

New salvation in Christ

The fourth assumption to challenge is that Paul believed salvation by faith was a new initiative of Christ. The problem here is the implication that "faith" equates only to "belief." Certainly Paul would not have recognised a Law in which it was sufficient to believe that God would save them. That was a promise that stood only as long as it was kept alive by covenant obedience.

Fittingly, Paul's message in Colossians appears to carry the same implications for life in Christ. It is not enough to only believe that Jesus died for the forgiveness of sins, the Colossians must "continue securely established and steadfast in the faith" (Col 1:23 cf. 2:5) in order to remain reconciled to him (Col 1:22). Paul revisits this theme in his contention with the Colossian deception, describing faith in terms of *participation* in the death of Christ in order to participate in the resurrection and renewal of humanity that is to be found in Christ (Col 2:12; 3:10). Faith (πίστις, pistis, Col 1:4, 23; 2:5, 7, 12), for Paul, is characterised by trust and so is no faith at all unless it is lived out as faithfulness, expressed in love (Col 1:4).[327] This, then, is remarkably close to the Old Covenant view of faith.

Legalistic Israel

Finally, we must confront the assumption that first-century Judaism was a legalistic religion.[328] As we have already discussed above, in light of E. P. Sanders and James Dunn,[329] it is clear that this was not the case. In fact, Sanders concluded that first-century Judaism had retained its emphasis on covenant relationship.[330] This relationship, founded on the assurance "I will be your God and you will be my people" (Lev 26:12), was maintained by God's continued faithfulness met with Israel's repentance and faith (cf. Mk 1:15). Accordingly,

---

[327] Dunn, *Colossians and Philemon*, 56-57; O'Brien, *Colossians, Philemon*, 11; Thompson, *Colossians and Philemon*, 19; Wright, *Colossians and Philemon*, 55; Martin, *Colossians and Philemon*, 48.

[328] Alexander, "Torah and Salvation in Tannaitic Literature" in *Justification and Variegated Nomism. Vol. 1: The Complexities of Second Temple Judaism* ; Cf. Zetterholm, *Approaches to Paul*, 101; Sanders, *Paul and Palestinian Judaism*, 33-59; Ziesler, *Pauline Christianity*, 103.

[329] Sanders, *Paul and Palestinian Judaism*, 233-38; Dunn, *Colossians and Philemon*, 30.

[330] Sanders, *Paul and Palestinian Judaism*, 236; cf. Ziesler, *Pauline Christianity*, 103.

obedience to the commandments of the Law was the appropriate response to the covenantal initiative Yahweh had taken. Sanders described this attitude as 'covenantal nomism', which he defined thus:

> Briefly, put, covenantal nomism is the view that one's place in God's plan is established on the basis of the covenant and that the covenant requires as the proper response of man his obedience to its commandments, while providing means of atonement for transgression.[331]

The heartbeat of first-century Judaism was not legalism but relationship, not concerned with earning God's favour but remaining within it.[332] As such, it is argued, Paul's primary concern was not to confront legalism, nor to object to a covenantal nomistic response to the Law. Indeed, he speaks of obedience to the Law as a measure for righteousness (Rom 2:13), which might equally be found in Gentiles if "what the law requires is written on their hearts" (Rom 2:14-15). Clearly this does not refer to the rituals, which Paul does not require Gentiles to perform (Rom 2:25-29; 1 Cor 8:8; Gal 5:2-6), but to the

---

[331] Sanders, *Paul and Palestinian Judaism*, 75.
[332] Dunn, *New Perspective*, 6; Thompson, *The New Perspective on Paul*, 8.

actions and attitudes of worship and lifestyle. Instead, Paul's aim was to clarify how the cross had redefined the central Jewish themes of covenant and election. Taking this as Paul's view, we would naturally expect these pillars of covenant and election, maintained by covenantal nomism, to be at the heart of Paul's presentation of life in Christ in Colossians.[333]

As well as recognising the significance of Paul's inclusion of Torah in the warning against deception, N. T. Wright notes the presence of two other major Jewish themes. Firstly, there is the Temple, which Wright connects to Paul's use of "in him" – just as God's presence dwells in the Temple, so "the fullness of deity dwells bodily" in Christ (Col 2:9; cf. 1:19). Therefore, those who are "faithful ministers of Christ" like Epaphras (Col 1:7) live and serve as priests "in Christ," the new covenant Temple. Secondly, there is circumcision, the first covenantal identifier of God's chosen people, which has been reimagined in light of the cross as discussed above. Taken together, we find that Paul is indeed adopting the key Jewish themes of covenant and election to describe the Colossians' salvation (from sin, Col 2:13-14; from spiritual opposition, Col 2:15) and new life (resurrection, Col 2:12) that has resulted from the cross.

---

[333] Cf. Donaldson, who claims that "Paul is to be understood as a covenantal nomist who came to believe that God had raised Jesus from the dead." Donaldson, *Paul and the Gentiles*, 51.

Relocating Law Into Christ

In doing so, Paul reminds the church where, or rather to whom, their faithfulness should be directed. Whereas, in the past, faithfulness was only possible for Jews since it was displayed by living according to the Law (Col 2:16, 21-22 cf. Deut 30:15-20; Jos 24:14; 1 Sam 26:23), now all may be faithful by living according to Christ (Col 2:8), in whom the Law is fulfilled (cf. Mt 5:17; Rom 10:4).

Whereas, in the past, faithfulness was protected by God's covenant with Israel, proven by the circumcision of Moses (Jn 7:22; Col 2:13; cf. Gen 17:10-14), now it is protected by the New Covenant (Jer 31:31; Lk 22:20), and proven by "the circumcision of Christ" (Col 2:11), displayed in baptism.[334]

Whereas, in the past, faithfulness was centred on the Temple, where God's presence dwelt (2 Chr 7:1-3, 12), now it is centred on Christ, in whom the fullness of God now dwells (Col 1:19; 2:9).[335] Having established this principle, Paul goes on to describe what this faithfulness will look like in practice (Col 3:5-4:1). The question remains, does this reflect an invitation into a covenantal nomistic faith, or does Paul present a different vision? It is to this question we now turn in the next chapter.

---

[334] Cf. Deuteronomy 10:16 – the circumcision of your heart. Paul is not introducing a new concept but building his covenantal theology on Scripture.

[335] Wright, *Paul and the Faithfulness of God*, 992-93; cf. Thompson, *Colossians and Philemon*, 54.

Chapter Fourteen
COVENANTAL EIKONISM

If Paul recognises the legitimacy of faithfulness to Yahweh expressed by a lifestyle of covenantal nomism, how far does he impress such behaviour on the Colossian Church? To answer this question, we need to look at Paul's discussion of life 'in Christ' from the perspective of what he promotes, not what he opposes.

While neither N. T. Wright nor Morna Hooker are suggesting that the deception referred to is unimportant, nor indeed do either offer an explanation that seeks to avoid discerning what it is, the shift they propose from imminent to potential threat is significant. It takes us away from the need to diagnose the problem for fear of not understanding the rest of the letter,[336] and releases us to focus, as Paul does, on the blessings already experienced by the Colossians as they live *in Christ*, in the face of temptation and alternative ideas.

---

[336] Contrary to Lincoln, *Colossians*, 561; and Moo, *Colossians and Philemon*, 49.

The Colossian Image

This positive emphasis is reinforced when we pay attention to the literary structure of the unit. As we ascertained in chapter five of this study, there is a chiastic system at work in Colossians 2:6-19, which has surprisingly been overlooked by scholars.[337]

The first indication that such a structure is in place is the presence of resonant key words in each half of the unit: πάσης ἀρχῆς καὶ ἐξουσίας (pases arches kai ezousias, "every ruler and authority," Col 2:10) is echoed by ἀρχὰς καὶ τὰς ἐξουσίας (archas kai tas ezousias, "rulers and authorities," Col 2:15); περιτομῇ (peritome, "circumcision," Col 2:11) corresponds to ἀκροβυστία (akrobystia, "uncircumcision," Col 2:13); παράδοσιν τῶν ἀνθρώπων (paradosin ton anthropon, "human tradition," Col 2:8) links conceptually to νοὸς τῆς σαρκὸς (noos tes sarkos, "human way of thinking," Col 2:18).

Then there is a potential association between στοιχεῖα τοῦ κόσμου (stoicheia tou kosmou, "elemental spirits of the universe," Col 2:8) and ἀγγέλων (aggelon, "angels," Col

---

[337] Dunn recognises a chiastic aspect to Colossians 2:8 as an introductory statement to the unit that follows, but fails to notice the chiasm in the unit as a whole, mainly because he, as others, considers Colossians 2: 6-7 to be a connecting phrase between units rather than the opening thought in a unit running Colossians 2:6-19, as I believe it is written. Cf. Dunn, *Colossians and Philemon*, 144.

2:18),³³⁸ as well as striking similarities of phraseology between "See to it that no one takes you captive" (2:8), "do not let anyone condemn you" (2:16), and "Do not let anyone disqualify you" (2:18). Finally, parallel metaphors pertaining to the state of the Church – initially utilising agricultural, industrial and legal language in 2:6-7 ("rooted," "built up," "established"), and then the more familiar 'body of Christ' metaphor in 2:19 – function as an inclusio for the unit. Piecing these correlating fragments together, a concentric system emerges that serves to push the deception to the edges and draw the supremacy of Christ, in relation to the redemption of humanity, into the centre (see Fig. L).³³⁹

---

³³⁸ Although other common interpretations include: 1) as mentioned in chapter twelve, στοιχεῖα ("elements") may also be translated as "basic principles" and so possibly stands an allusion to the Law, not to astral powers; 2) Alternatively, it may refer simply to the material astral bodies of stars and planets: Lucas, *The Message of Colossians and Philemon*, 113; 3) Or else it may refer to the Greek philosophical use of "elements," concerning the composition of creation from fire, earth, water and air: Thompson, *Colossians and Philemon*, 52.

³³⁹ There is a potential weakness with this observation, namely that it lacks balance, with the C' and B' strophes being longer than any of the others. Nevertheless, given the repeated use of chiastic systems throughout the letter, as well as the definite echoing of vocabulary and themes that mirror one another here, it seems likely that there is a chiastic intent within this unit. However, this remains an area of Colossian studies that warrants further research.

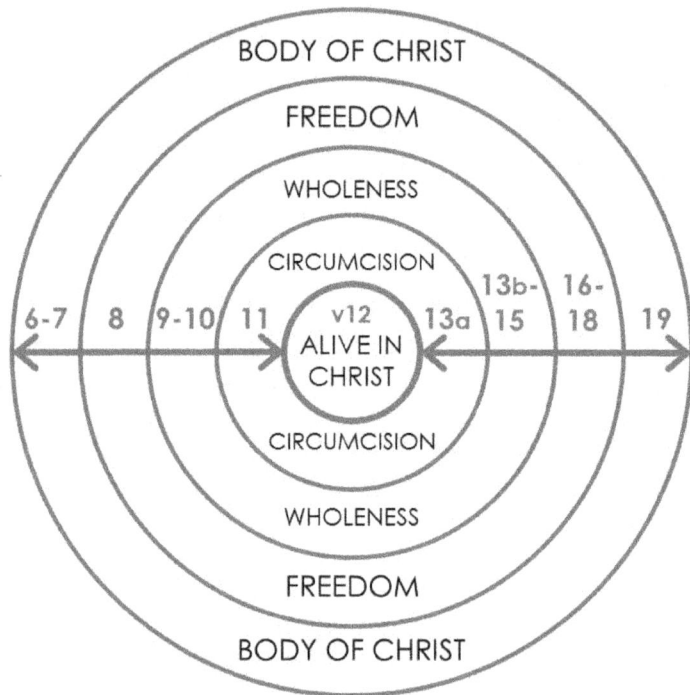

Fig. L – Colossians 2:6-19 chiasmus

This chiastic structure reinforces where the heart of Paul's argument lies. Not in his opposition to any threat (which surely exists, but is peripheral to the chiasmus), but in his assertion of the centrality of the death and resurrection of Christ, not only as the object of the Colossians' faith but as the pinnacle moment in which they participate. This assurance of resurrection is

Covenantal Eikonism

ultimately attained by baptism, but is approached by rejecting the ways of the world (be that Law or other syncretistic issues) that had formerly barred the Colossians from becoming God's chosen people, and entering into the new covenant through "circumcision in Christ," which is completed on the cross.[340]

Consistent with the foundations of a covenantal nomistic religion, Paul points to the source of God's grace (2:12) and reminds the Colossians that they have already attained fullness (2:10), and will continue to live in it as long as they continue to place their faith in Christ and not anything or anyone else (2:16-18). What then follows in 3:5-17 is a list of behaviours to avoid (which are acts of disobedience, Col 3:6) and to adopt (as God's chosen ones, Col 3:12). Thus the issues of covenant and election are maintained in Paul's practical analysis of what life 'in Christ' should look like.[341]

The first indication that covenantal nomism is *not* what Paul has in mind is the position of covenantal references in Paul's chiasm. Having pushed the demands of the Sinaitic covenant to the edges, he draws the Abrahamic covenant demand of circumcision to the centre (Gen 17:4-

---

[340] Thompson, *Colossians and Philemon*, 61; Dunn, *Colossians and Philemon*, 159.
[341] O'Brien, *Colossians, Philemon*, 176.

14). Paul affects a similar shift in Galatians (Gal 3:6-9),[342] stating that Christ died to restore the blessings of Abraham to all who have faith in Christ (Gal 3:13-14, 27-29).[343] In this scheme, the Sinaitic covenant is presented as a temporary covering until Christ can initiate the permanent solution (Gal 3:23-26). The closeness of language with Colossians, including clothing as a baptismal image (Gal 3:27 cf. Col 3:10, 12, 14) and a vision of a united, equal humanity (Gal 3:28 cf. Col 3:11), surely invites the same interpretation.[344]

When we examine the Abrahamic covenant we find a close thematic connection to humanity's commission as the image of God (Gen 1:26-28), according to the 'eikonic' blessings we identified in chapter three – namely, that humanity shares an intimate communion with God, and unity within itself, through which it exercises life-giving power (fruitfulness) in and authority over creation.

Out of a covenant relationship with God (communion), Abraham becomes "the ancestor of a multitude of

---

[342] I have argued in a previous paper that he does the same in Romans 9-11. See: Hedley, 'Romans 9-11 and Israel in the New Covenant', which I have made available for download on my Academia profile (www.academia.edu/8400066/Romans_9-11_and_Israel_in_the_New_Covenant).
[343] Longenecker, *Galatians*, 110-12.
[344] Barclay, *Colossians and Philemon*, 87, 110; Dunn, *Colossians and Philemon*, 160; Connell, "Clothing the Body of Christ," *Worship* 135; Longenecker, *Galatians*, 156-57.

Covenantal Eikonism

nations" and "exceedingly fruitful" (life-giving power, Gen 17:5-6), and he is promised possession of the land of Canaan (authority, Gen 17:8). This covenant is then extended beyond a personal relationship to a corporate human one (unity), in which circumcision unites master with slave, the elect with the foreigner, father with son, and all generations (Gen 17:12-13). This final picture of unity is clearly in view in Colossians 3:11, which mirrors the delineation of people by ethnicity and status to draw a direct connection between the renewal of humanity as God's image and the establishment of a (new) covenant relationship with God (cf. Jer 31:31-34; Eze 11:17-20; Lk 22:20), which is no longer defined by fleshly circumcision:

> Throughout your generations *every male among you* shall be circumcised when he is eight days old, *including the slave born* in your house and the one bought with your money *from any foreigner* who is not of your offspring.
> Genesis 17:12

> In that renewal there is *no longer Greek and Jew*, circumcised and uncircumcised, *barbarian, Scythian, slave and free*, but Christ is all and in all!
> Colossians 3:11

The Colossian Image

Unity is a key theme throughout Colossians 3:5-4:1,[345] which concludes with a Haustafel showing a number of social relationships reimagined with unity at their foundation (Col 3:18-4:1). In fact, on closer examination, we find each relationship defined by the eikonic hallmarks that Paul envisages characterising this new humanity.

In each case, life is depicted as rooted in the Lord (communion, Col 3:18, 20, 22, 23, 24; 4:1), which leads to authority, which has been radically reimagined according to circumstance. In positions of influence, authority is exercised as love (Col 3:19), gentleness (Col 3:21), and justice (Col 4:1). When in positions of subordination, it is exercised as submission (Col 3:18), obedience (Col 3:20, 22), and perseverance (Col 3:23). This reflects clearly the authority of Christ, which carries the same power in his strength as in his weakness on the cross.

The impact of this unity, communion and authority is life-giving power, displayed in terms of honour (Col 3:19), encouragement (Col 3:21), purpose (Col 3:23), inheritance (Col 3:24) and justice (Col 4:1). Thus, what is in view is not humanity living as the renewed people of Sinai but as the renewed image of God (cf. Col 3:10).[346] In which case, Paul's understanding of Christian faithfulness is not ultimately expressed as 'covenantal nomism' (following

---

[345] Barclay, *Colossians and Philemon*, 88.
[346] Thompson, *Colossians and Philemon*, 78.

Covenantal Eikonism

the Law in response to God's covenantal initiative), but as 'covenantal eikonism', living as the renewed image of God in response to Christ's covenantal initiative on the cross: sharing communion with God's indwelling Spirit, exercising His authority to bear the fruit of life-giving love, and pursuing the reunification of humanity across all its dividing lines.

This is not to suggest that covenantal nomism should be reassessed as a reality of first century Judaism, nor that it cannot stand as a faithful Christian response to the New Covenant in Christ. I have already pointed to the work of E. P. Sanders, James Dunn and others to emphasise the importance of rediscovering covenantal nomism as the spiritual context into which the first-century Church is born, to show that Paul is not countering legalism, nor is he claiming Christianity as a new expression of faithfulness; rather, he is already familiar with the covenantal-relational emphasis of the Old Testament and draws it into his vision for renewed humanity.

However, while covenantal nomism may inform Paul's perspective, it is insufficient to satisfy his hope, which envisions a total reconfiguring of the whole of humanity (Col 3:9-11). Not that he rejects it, but he redefines it in the light of Christ within the wider scope of restoration conveyed by covenantal eikonism. At the heart of covenantal nomism is the ritual practice of circumcision and willing obedience to the Torah, and it is these very elements that Paul specifies have been relocated to Christ (2:6-23). Thus covenantal nomism may stand as a faithful expression of covenantal eikonism, as long as those aspects of Law that govern election and the administration of God's grace are understood to have been relocated into Christ, and the life that emerges reflects the transformation, authorisation, and love of the renewed image of God (Col 3:12-4:1).

A key signpost to this difference in perspective at the heart of Paul's message to the Colossians is the paucity of references to the Law in the second half of his letter. Links certainly can be made with the first list of "earthly" sins (Col 3:5), which loosely correspond to the Ten Commandments (cf. Ex 20:1-17) and are described in legal terms of disobedience (Col 3:6). Correspondingly, the attribution of the Church as "chosen ones, holy and beloved" (Col 3:12) echoes God's words to Israel at Sinai: "If you obey my voice and keep my covenant you shall be my treasured possession ... you shall be for me a priestly kingdom and a holy nation" (Ex 19:5-6).[347] However, the majority of Paul's warnings and exhortations cannot be satisfactorily understood in terms of the Law.

---

[347] Douglas Moo points to this being a familiar Old Testament pattern, and identifies a number of further correlations (1 Chr 16:13; Pss 105:6, 43; 106:5; Wis 4:15; Isa 43:20; 45:4; 65:9): Moo, *Colossians and Philemon*, 275.

Covenantal Eikonism

Whereas, here again we find a resolution by reading this section in the light of the Abrahamic covenant and its correlation to the hallmarks of the image of God found in Genesis 1:26-28. The same eikonic characteristics that populate the Genesis 17 blessing make up the substance of Paul's presentation of life 'in Christ'.[348] Paul warns against any practice that breaks covenant relationship (communion) through idolatry (Col 3:5), or is harmful to life and undermining of authority (Col 3:8), or is disunifying (Col 3:9). These stand as the direct antithesis to the image of God blessings. In their place, Paul depicts a life in covenant relationship with God – "chosen ones, holy and beloved" (as already noted above, this reflects the covenant declaration of Yahweh over His people at Sinai, Ex 19:5-6) – in which the Church creates life through love and forgiveness (Col 3:13-14),[349] and exercises authority with humility (Col 3:12).[350]

Ralph Martin describes this as "Paul's intention to hold up the divine character as a sublime model and to encourage his Colossian friends to catch the divine

---

[348] A similar comparison may be made with the pre-covenant promises of Genesis 12:1-3 and the first covenant struck with Abram in Genesis 15.
[349] Weiss discusses the life-giving emphasis of forgiveness: Weiss, *The Law in the Epistle to the Colossians*, 310; Cf. Barclay, *Colossians and Philemon*, 89.
[350] Martin, *Colossians and Philemon*, 111.

spirit."[351] In other words, in response to the grace of God that has renewed humanity (Col 3:10), humanity is called to do what God does, just as God's image was called in creation. After all, what had God spent the previous six days doing before creating His image, if not communing among Himself ("Let us ...," Gen 1:26), as a united community,[352] subduing the earth ("And God said ... and it was so"), and creating life? Reinforcing this, Paul describes the foundation of this reconfigured life as the indwelling presence and influence of Christ (cf. Col 2:10),[353] who confers peace (i.e. fullness of life, Col 3:15), word (which inspires a worshipful communion with God, Col 3:16), and commission (through which they exercise the authority of heaven, Col 3:17).

This connection with the themes of the Abrahamic and Adamic covenants draws us back from the localised problem of Israel's rebellion against the Sinai covenant to the more fundamental problem of humanity's rebellion against their creation as the image of God.[354] Hence the prominence of Adam Christology in the letter, importing

---

[351] Martin, *Colossians and Philemon*, 111-12.
[352] Note the plural sense of God's name אֱלֹהִים (Elohim), which literally means "gods," except that the singular nature of the corresponding verb בְּרָא (bara, "created") determines that Elohim must also be singular.
[353] As per Weiss, *The Law in the Epistle to the Colossians*, 313; Martin, *Colossians and Philemon*, 80.
[354] Cf. Wright, *Paul: Fresh Perspectives*, 24.

Covenantal Eikonism

the eikonic blessings given to Adam into Christ,[355] and Paul's emphasis on the ultimate effect of the cross, which is given full voice in the central statement of his practical vision for life in Christ: they have stripped off the old humanity (Col 3:9), and with it their former fallen nature and the law to counter its effects, and put on the new humanity, which is "renewed in knowledge according to the image of its creator" (Col 3:10).[356]

This, then, is the heart of Paul's message. As Christians participate in Christ's death and resurrection in baptism (Col 2:12) they are raised with him and become what he is: the image of God (Col 1:15).[357] In response to this astonishing act of God's grace, the call of the church is to a life of covenantal eikonism, living according to the hallmarks of the image of God as the evidence of their reconciliation to God in the New Covenant.

---

[355] Seyoon Kim, *The Origin of Paul's Gospel* (Grand Rapids: Eerdmans, 1981), 137; Wall, *Colossians and Philemon*, 142; Dunn, *Colossians and Philemon*, 221-22.

[356] As this implies, there may also be a chiastic structure to this unit. Certainly there is a loose chiasm at work, with Col 3:10-11 standing as the central statement that holds together the two halves of the overall unit, which discuss the lifestyle of the world (Col 3:5-9) and the lifestyle of heaven (Col 3:12-17). However, beyond this any closer chiasm is elusive and may not be present.

[357] Hooker, *Paul*, 103; Cf. Dunn, *Colossians and Philemon*, 161.

Chapter Fifteen

EIKONIC LIFE IN CHRIST

Having now carefully analysed the book and its themes, we are in a position to summarise and reflect on the conclusions that have emerged. Colossians has often been heralded as a key text for understanding the developing theology and practice of the early Church.[358] While the majority of scholarly energy has been devoted to reading the letter through the lens of its high Christology, the aim of this book has been to turn the scope around and assess how such a high Christology impacts the humanity it sees; in particular, how the movement from Christ as the image of God (Col 1:15) to humanity bearing that same image (Col 3:10) affects how we understand humanity's place in God's kingdom and how this shapes Paul's presentation of Christian life "in Christ." This assessment has unfolded in three stages.

---

[358] E.g., Thompson, *Colossians and Philemon*, 1; Barclay, *Colossians and Philemon*, 11; Dunn, *Colossians and Philemon*, 19.

First, by undertaking a close reading of the letter to survey its portrayal of humanity, we have seen the importance of anthropology as a key theological theme throughout the letter, which is closely associated with its more celebrated Christology. This anthropology is rooted in a narrative of redemption (Col 1:13-14), reconciliation (Col 1:20-23) and recreation (Col 2:10-12; 3:5-17), which draws humanity alongside Christ to participate in his death and resurrection (Col 2:12; 3:1) as it submits to Christ as Lord, enters into baptism and conforms its life to Christ.[359] What emerges is a new humanity, which lives by faith, love, and hope (Col 1:4-5) and shares in the blessings associated with Christ's image identity, which convey the fullness of the presence of God (Col 2:10; 3:16 cf. Col 1:19; 2:9), life-giving power of resurrection (Col 2:12-13; 3:1 cf. Col 1:18), authority (Col 2:10; 3:18-4:1 cf. Col 1:16; 2:15), and unity (Col 3:11; 3:14 cf. Col 1:17).

Second, by reflecting on the implications of the evocative use of "image" language, we have found that this four-fold portrayal of true humanity is held together by Paul's theology of the image of God, which simultaneously draws on cultural and religious significance to present a renewed human identity whose allegiance is to the lordship of Jesus and no other; and

---

[359] Cf. Richard Hays' argument for a narrative substructure running through Paul's theology: Hays, *The Faith of Jesus Christ*, 28.

whose worship is directed towards Christ as Wisdom, the divine agent of creation. This emphasis on creation also naturally draws our gaze to view the image of God in connection to humanity's original design (Gen 1:26-28). Here we find Christ associated with a humanity that bears the same hallmarks of God's indwelling presence (צֶלֶם, Gen 1:26 cf. εἰκων, Col 1:15), unity ("male and female," Gen 1:27 cf. "all things," Col 1:17), authority ("dominion," "subdue," Gen 1:26, 28 cf. Christ's authority, Col 1:16; 2:10, 15), and life-giving power ("be fruitful and multiply," Gen 1:28 cf. resurrection, Col 1:18) that are at the heart of the Genesis 1 human commission.

In the hands of the pre-eminent Christ, however, these hallmarks are as much a feature of his divinity as his humanity. Thus, the movement of Colossians is towards an inaugurated eschatology, in which humanity is renewed as the image of God according to Christ's exalted prototype (Col 3:10 cf. 1:15), such that its heavenly future is not only assured but may be drawn ever more tangibly into its earthly present.[360]

Finally, we have found that this renewal takes root as Christians enter into life "in Christ" (Col 2:6, 7), in order to reflect the true humanity of Christ. Here again we find a movement from Christ to humanity as God's people

---

[360] Cf. Dunn, *Colossians and Philemon*, 36; Wall, *Colossians and Philemon*, 18; O'Brien, *Colossians, Philemon*, xlvi.

participate in the 'in him' assurances of Christ's authority (Col 1:16 cf. 2:10), fullness (Col 1:19 cf. Col 2:10), and resurrection (Col 1:18 cf. 2:12). Paul describes this as entering into "the circumcision of Christ" (Col 2:11), which results in a New Covenant relationship as Christ sets aside the Sinaitic covenant identifiers of circumcision (Col 2:12), the Law (Col 2:14), and food laws (Col 2:16), and replaces them with the invitation to be circumcised in him (Col 2:11), in order to fully realise the promise of the Abrahamic covenant.

Just as the Sinaitic covenant was an act of God's grace that was entered into by repentance and faith, so the New Covenant is enacted in the same way. However, whereas the faith required in the Sinaitic covenant was best characterised as 'covenantal nomism' (following the law in response to God's covenantal initiative), the faith Paul describes is better defined as 'covenantal eikonism': living as the image of God in response to Christ's covenantal initiative. Nevertheless, there is nothing necessarily to bar covenantal nomism as a faithful expression of covenantal eikonism, so long as those aspects of Law that govern election and the administration of God's grace are understood to have been relocated into Christ.

Indeed, with this caveat in place, there is little to differentiate nomism from eikonism, because ultimately it amounts to the same thing: responding in repentance and faith to the source of God's grace. This call to covenantal eikonism finds its final and fullest expression in Colossians 3:5-4:1, as Paul accompanies his invitation into a renewed humanity (Col 3:10) with a detailed rendition of what such a renewed existence looks like in practice. Here we find a vision for Christian life that reflects the same four hallmarks of the image of God that have been established throughout the letter, and so Paul leaves his readers with a vision of the fullness of new humanity that has been received through its participation in Christ.

Implications of the study

While a great deal of scholarship has been devoted to unpacking the Christology of Colossians, and its implications for humanity, comparatively little attention has been directed towards the nature of humanity itself. As we have seen, this is a rich theme throughout the letter, with a narrative understanding of humanity's original creation, fall, redemption and transformation into the renewed image of God, blended with a developed liturgical presence administrating the entrance into this new humanity, and a clear understanding of how faithfulness to Christ, expressed as 'covenantal eikonism', maintains this position. Thus, this study contributes to our understanding of how the early church saw its role within Christ's kingdom and place within new creation.

The Colossian Image

To this end, I have argued that a correlation between life 'in Christ' and the renewal of humanity as the image of God indicates the development of a high anthropology in the early church, rooted in an advanced Christology, encompassing both the high notes of Christ's divinity and the low notes of his humanity. Such an anthropological perspective clearly has relevance for the life of the Church today, as it emphasises the critical role God's people carry in Christ's continued mission to renew the whole of humanity. Moreover, it affirms the freedom of all followers of Christ to live according to the hallmarks of God's image, embracing the indwelling of the Spirit, exercising the power and authority of God, and pursuing unity, as part of a lifestyle that seeks to reflect Christ more and see his kingdom come on earth as it is in heaven (Mt 6:10).

Further to this, although my argument has not relied on Paul as the author of the epistle, I believe that the high anthropology and vision for covenantal eikonism that underpins Colossians forms a similar foundational theme in other Pauline sources, most notably Romans, 1 and 2 Corinthians, and Ephesians.[361] Contrary to Anthony Thiselton's claim that "Paul does not set out a coherent view of humanity," my belief is that his letter to the

---

[361] Thus, following the deliberate ambiguity of Barclay, I refer to Pauline here in its broadest sense, reflecting a school of Pauline thought: Barclay, *Colossians and Philemon*, 77.

Colossians does precisely this, and that where we find similar 'eikonic' foundations in play elsewhere in Pauline literature we can argue for a similar coherence.[362]

Key indicators that just such foundations may be present are, as we have seen throughout this study, a vision of life "in Christ" – itself a very common Pauline theme that features in every Pauline epistle except 2 Thessalonians and Titus – combined with any or all of the following: references to a new identity (Rom 7:6; 1 Cor 5:7; 2 Cor 5:17; Gal 6:15; Eph 2:15; 4:24), language that specifically evokes the image of God either for Christ (2 Cor 4:4) or humanity (Rom 8:29; 1 Cor 15:49; 2 Cor 3:18), or explicit Adam Christology (Rom 5:12-21; 1 Cor 15:22, 45). Thus I hope that the exposition and argument in this study may be of benefit to wider Pauline studies.

Areas for further research

As the above comments attest, there is significant scope for a wider study of high anthropology and its relationship to Christian faithfulness expressed as covenantal eikonism in relation to Pauline literature. Such a study would be instructive to three key aspects of Pauline scholarship. Firstly, it would contribute a new perspective to the Pauline treatment of humanity and the

---

[362] Thiselton, *The Living Paul*, 67.

image of God, and their place as key themes within the soteriological, eschatological and ecclesiological arguments that dominate Pauline epistles. In view of this, I have tried to make connections throughout this study to other correlating passages in the Pauline corpus, but limitations of space and time have precluded any more extensive study of these issues here.

Secondly, by identifying and developing key thematic correlations between these aspects in Colossians and elsewhere in the Pauline corpus, it may make a valuable contribution to the ongoing analysis of the authorship of Colossians. This is an aspect I have steered clear of in this study, lest it become a distraction from establishing the internal logic of my Colossian argument. However, while nothing raised in this study can point indisputably to the work of Paul's own hand, as opposed to a broader Pauline school of thought, the establishment of close anthropological correlations between Colossians and other undisputed epistles may at least add weight to the call not to dismiss Paul's authorship on the basis of theological divergence.[363]

Finally, the emphasis I have placed on the literary structure of the letter feeds into what is very much a live topic within Pauline scholarship, especially with regard to the interpolation of hymns, creeds, and baptismal liturgy

---

[363] Cf. Wright, *Colossians and Philemon*, 36-37; O'Brien, *Colossians, Philemon*, xlix.

that contribute to the overall argument of the letter. Where this study may add to that discussion is in the importance given to an undergirding structure of repeating chiastic units that draw the reader in to the key components of the argument. Although chiastic traces have often been found, I believe this study goes further by recognising a device that is employed consistently through the letter and directly contributes to the message of the whole. Here again, there has been limited space to develop this scheme as fully as could be envisaged, and this is certainly an area that would benefit from further independent attention.

BIBLIOGRAPHY OF CITED WORKS

Achtemeier, Paul J. *Romans: Interpretation, A Bible Commentary for Teaching and Preaching.* Louisville: Westminster John Knox, 2010.

Alexander, P. S. "Torah and Salvation in Tannaitic Literature." Pages 261-301 in *Justification and Variegated Nomism. Vol. 1: The Complexities of Second Temple Judaism.* Edited by D. A. Carson, Peter T. O'Brien and Mark A. Seifrid. Tubingen: Mohr Siebeck, 2001.

Arnold, Clinton E. *The Colossian Syncretism.* Tubingen: Mohr Siebeck, 1995.

Athanasius. "On The Incarnation Of The Word." Pages 249-335 in *NPNF 2-04.* Edited by Philip Schaff. Grand Rapids: Christian Classics Ethereal Library, n.d.

Atkinson, David. *The Message of Genesis 1-11.* Leicester: Inter Varsity Press, 1990.

Avrahami, Yael. *The Senses of Scripture: Sensory Perception in the Hebrew Bible.* London: Bloomsbury, 2012.

Bandstra, A. J. *The Law and the Elements of the World.* Kampen: J. H. Kok, 1964.

Barclay, John M. G. *Colossians and Philemon.* London: T & T Clark, 2004.

—. "Paul Among the Diaspora Jews: Anomaly or Apostate?" *Journal for the Study of the New Testament* 60(1995): 89-120.

—. "Paul, Judaism, and the Jewish People." Pages 188-201 in *The Blackwell Companion to Paul*. Edited by Stephen Westerholm. Malden: Wiley-Blackwell, 2011.

—. *Pauline Churches and Diaspora Jews*. Tübingen: Mohr, 2011.

Barrett, C. K. *Paul: An Introduction To His Thought*. Louisville: Westminster John Knox Press, 1994.

Barth, Karl. *Church Dogmatics III.I*. Edinburgh: T & T Clark, 1960.

Barth, Markus, and Helmut Blanke. *Colossians: A New Translation with Introduction and Commentary*. New Haven: Yale University Press, 1994.

Barthelemy, Jean-Dominique. *God and His Image: An Outline of Biblical Theology*. San Francisco: Ignatius Press, 2007.

Beetham, Christopher A. *Echoes of Scripture in the Letter of Paul to the Colossians*. Leiden: Society of Biblical Literature, 2008.

Bird, Michael F., ed. *Four Views On The Apostle Paul*. Grand Rapids: Zondervan, 2012.

Blackwell, Ben C. "You Are Filled In Him: Theosis and Colossians 2-3." *Journal of Theological Interpretation* 8, no. 1(2014): 103-124.

Bornkamm, Gunther. "The Heresy of Colossians." Pages 123-45 in *Conflict at Colossae: A Problem in the Interpretation of Early Christianity Illustrated by Selected Modern Studies*. Edited by Fred O. Francis and

Bibliography

Wayne A. Meeks. Missoula: Society of Biblical Literature, 1975.

Bruce, F. F. "Christ as Conqueror and Reconciler." *Bibliotheca Sacra* 141, no. 564(1984): 291-302.

—. "The Colossian Heresy." *Bibliotheca Sacra* 141, no. 563(1984): 195-208.

Brueggemann, Walter. *Genesis: Interpretation, A Bible Commentary for Teaching and Preaching.* Atlanta: John Knox Press, 1982.

Campbell, Douglas A. "Christ and the Church in Paul: A 'Post-New Perspective' Account." Pages 113-143 in *Four Views on the Apostle Paul.* Edited by Michael F. Bird. Grand Rapids: Zondervan, 2012.

Carter, Warren. "Paul and the Roman Empire: Recent Perspectives." Pages 7-26 in *Paul Unbound: Other Perspectives on the Apostle.* Edited by Mark D. Given. Peabody: Hendrickson, 2010.

Connell, Martin F. "Clothing the Body of Christ: An Inquiry about the Letters of Paul." *Worship* 85(2011): 128-46.

Corley, Bruce C. "Jews, the Future, and God (Romans 9-11)." *Southwestern Journal of Theology* 19(1976): 42-56.

Daly, Robert J. "Images of God and the Imitation of God: Problems with Atonement." *Theological Studies* 68, no. 1(2007): 36-51.

Deissmann, Adolf. *Light From The Ancient East: The New Testament Illustrated By Recently Discovered Texts Of The Graeco-Roman World.* Translated by

Lionel R. M. Strachan. London: Hodder and Stoughton, 1927.

DeMaris, R. E. *The Colossian Controversy: Wisdom in Dispute at Colossae (Journal for the Study of the New Testament: Supplement).* Vol. 96. Sheffield: Continuum, 1994.

Dibelius, Martin. "The Isis Initiation in Apuleius and Related Initiatory Rites." Pages 61-121 in *Conflict at Colossae: A Problem in the Interpretation of Early Christianity Illustrated by Selected Modern Studies.* Edited by Fred O. Francis and Wayne A. Meeks. Missoula: Society of Biblical Literature, 1975.

Donaldson, Terence L. *Paul and the Gentiles: Remapping the Apostle's Convictional World.* Minneapolis: Fortress Press, 1997.

Dunn, James D. G. *Jesus, Paul and the Law: Studies in Mark and Galatians.* SPCK, 1990.

—. *The Epistles to the Colossians and to Philemon: A Commentary on the Greek Text.* Grand Rapids: Eerdmans, 1996.

—. *The New Perspective on Paul.* Grand Rapids: Eerdmans, 2007.

—. *The Theology of Paul the Apostle.* Grand Rapids: Eerdmans, 1998.

Eisenberg, Ronald L. *The 613 Mitzvot: A Contemporary Guide to the Commandments of Judaism.* Rockville: Schreiber Publishing, 2005.

Bibliography

Elliott, Neil. "Paul and the Politics of Empire: Problems and Prospects." Pages 17-39 in *Paul and Politics: Ekklesia, Israel, Imperium, Interpretation.* Edited by Richard A. Horsley. Harrisburgh: Trinity Press International, 2000.

Fee, Gordon D. *1 and 2 Timothy, Titus.* Grand Rapids: Baker Books, 1988.

—. *Paul, the Spirit, and the People of God.* Grand Rapids: Baker Academic, 1996.

—. *Pauline Christology: An Exegetical Theological Study.* Peabody: Hendrickson Publishers, 2007.

Fletcher-Louis, Crispin. "God's Image, His Cosmic Temple and the High Priest: Towards an Historical and Theological Account of the Incarnation." Pages 81-100 in *Heaven on Earth: The Temple in Biblical Theology.* Edited by S. Gathercole and T. D. Alexander. Paternoster, 2004.

Francis, Fred O. "Humility and Angelic Worship in Col 2:18." Pages 163-195 in *Conflict at Colossae: A Problem in the Interpretation of Early Christianity Illustrated by Selected Modern Studies.* Edited by Fred O. Francis and Wayne A. Meeks. Missoula: Society of Biblical Literature, 1975.

—. "The Background of Embateuein (Col 2:18) in Legal Papyri and Oracle Inscriptions." Pages 197-207 in *Conflict at Colossae: A Problem in the Interpretation of Early Christianity Illustrated by Selected Modern Studies.* Edited by Fred O. Francis and Wayne A. Meeks. Missoula: Society of Biblical Literature, 1975.

Garland, David E. *Colossians and Philemon: The NIV Application Commentary.* Grand Rapids: Zondervan, 1988.

Georgi, Dieter. *Theocracy In Paul's Practice and Theology.* Translated by D. E. Green. Minneapolis: Fortress Press, 1991.

Gorman, Michael. *Apostle of the Crucified Lord: a Theological Introduction to Paul and his Letters.* Grand Rapids: Eerdmans, 2004.

—. *Inhabiting the Cruciform God: Kenosis, Justification, and Theosis in Paul's Narrative Soteriology.* Grand Rapids: Eerdmans, 2009.

—. *Reading Paul.* Eugene: Cascade Books, 2008.

Hamilton, Victor P. *The Book Of Genesis, Chapters 1-17.* Grand Rapids: Eerdmans, 1990.

Harink, Douglas. *Paul Among the Postliberals: Pauline Theology Beyond Christendom and Modernity.* Eugene: Wipf and Stock, 2003.

Hay, David M. "Pistis as "Ground for Faith" in Hellenized Judaism and Paul." *Journal of Biblical Literature* 108(1989): 461-76.

Hays, Richard B. *Echoes of Scripture in the Letters of Paul.* New Haven: Yale University Press, 1989.

—. *The Faith of Jesus Christ: an Investigation of the Narrative Substructure of Galatians 3:1-4:11.* Chico: Scholars Press, 1983.

Bibliography

Hedley, Freddy. *The God of Page One: Rediscovering God's Identity and Ours.* Emblem, 2012.

—. "Romans 9-11 and Israel in the New Covenant." Cheltenham: Westminster Theological Centre, 2013.

Heisey, Nancy R. "Paul on Idolatry: Finding Fruitful Fellowship." *Vision* 12, no. 1(2011): 43-50.

Hooker, Morna D. *Paul: A Short Introduction.* London: Oneworld Publications, 2003.

—. "Were There False Teachers in Colossae?" Pages 315-331 in *Christ and Spirit in the New Testament: Studies in Honour of Charles Francis Digby Moule.* Edited by Barnabas Lindars and Stephen S. Smalley. Cambridge: Cambridge University Press, 1973.

Horrell, David G. *An Introduction to the Study of Paul (second edition).* New York: T&T Clark, 2006.

Horsley, Richard A., ed. *Paul and Empire: Religion and Power in Roman Imperial Society.* London: Continuum, 1997.

Jervell, Jacob. *The Unknown Paul: Essays on Luke-Acts and Early Christian History.* Grand Rapids: Fortress Press, 1984.

Johnson, David H. "The Image of God in Colossians." *Didaskalia* 3, no. 2(1992): 9-15.

Johnson, S. Lewis. "The Paralysis of Legalism." *Bibliotheca Sacra* 120, no. 478(1963): 109-16.

Käsemann, Ernst. "A Primitive Christian Baptismal Liturgy." Pages 149-68 in *Essays on New Testament Themes*. London: SCM Press, 1964.

Keck, Leander E. *Paul And His Letters*. Philadelphia: Fortress Press, 1988.

Kidner, Derek. *Genesis: An Introduction and Commentary*. Leicester: Inter Varsity Press, 1967.

Kilner, John Frederic. "Humanity in God's Image: Is the Image Really Damaged?" *Journal of the Evangelical Theological Society* 53, no. 3(2010): 601-17.

Kim, Seyoon. *Paul and the New Perspective: Second Thoughts on the Origin of Paul's Gospel*. Grand Rapids: Eerdmans, 2002.

—. *The Origin of Paul's Gospel*. Grand Rapids: Eerdmans, 1981.

Kirk, J. R. Daniel. *Jesus I Have Loved, But Paul?* Grand Rapids: Baker Academic, 2011.

Kreitzer, L. Joseph. "Christ and Second Adam in Paul." *Communio viatorum* 32, no. 1-2(1989): 55-101.

Kruse, Colin G. *2 Corinthians: An Introduction and Commentary*. Nottingham: Inter-Varsity Press, 2008.

Lightfoot, J. B. "The Colossian Heresy." Pages 13-59 in *Conflict at Colossae: A Problem in the Interpretation of Early Christianity Illustrated by Selected Modern Studies*. Edited by Fred O. Francis and Wayne A. Meeks. Missoula: Society of Biblical Literature, 1975.

Bibliography

Lincoln, Andrew T. "The Letter to the Colossians: Introduction, Commentary, and Reflections." Pages 551-669 in *The New Interpreter's Bible, Volume XI.* Edited by Leander E. Keck. Nashville: Abingdon Press, 2000.

Lohse, Eduard. *Colossians and Philemon: Hermeneia, A Critical and Historical Commentary.* Minneapolis: Fortress Press, 1971.

Longenecker, Richard N. *Galatians: Word Biblical Commentary 41.* Nashville: Thomas Nelson, 1990.

—., ed. *The Road from Damascus: The Impact of Paul's Conversion on His Life, Thought and Ministry.* Grand Rapids: Eerdmans, 1997.

Lucas, Dick. *The Message of Colossians and Philemon: Fullness and Freedom.* Downers Grove: Inter-Varsity Press, 1980.

Lyonnet, Stanislas. "Paul's Adversaries in Colossae." Pages 147-161 in *Conflict at Colossae: A Problem in the Interpretation of Early Christianity Illustrated by Selected Modern Studies.* Edited by Fred O. Francis and Wayne A. Meeks. Missoula: Society of Biblical Literature, 1975.

Maier, Harry O. "A Sly Civility: Colossians and Empire." *Journal for the Study of the New Testament* 27, no. 3(2005): 323-49.

—. *Picturing Paul in Empire: Imperial Image, Text and Persuasion in Colossians, Ephesians and the Pastoral Epistles.* London: T & T Clark, 2013.

Marcus, Joel. "Idolatry in the New Testament." *Interpretation* 60, no. 2(2006): 152-64.

Martin, Ralph P. "Aspects of Worship in the New Testament Church." *Vox Evangelica* 2(1963): 6-32.

—. *Colossians and Philemon: New Century Bible Commentary.* Grand Rapids: Eerdmans, 1981.

Martin, Troy W. *By Philosophy and Empty Deceit: Colossians as Response toa Cynic Critique.* Sheffield: Sheffield Academic Press, 1996.

McCasland, S. Vernon. ""The Image of God" According to Paul." *Journal of Biblical Literature* 69, no. 2(1950): 85-100.

Middleton, J. Richard. *A New Heaven And A New Earth: Reclaiming Biblical Eschatology.* Grand Rapids: Baker Academic, 2014.

—. *The Liberating Image: The Imago Dei in Genesis 1.* Grand Rapids: Brazos Press, 2005.

Moberly, R. W. L. *The Theology of the Book of Genesis.* Cambridge: Cambridge University Press, 2009.

Montgomery, Eric. "The Image of God as the Resurrected State in Pauline Thought." *Bible.Org* 11 March 2005. <https://bible.org/article/image-god-resurrected-state-pauline-thought>.

Moo, Douglas J. *The Epistle to the Romans.* Grand Rapids: Eerdmans, 1996.

Bibliography

—. *The Letters to the Colossians and to Philemon (Pillar New Testament Commentaries)*. Downers Grove: Inter Varsity Press, 2008.

Moyise, Steve. *Paul and Scripture: Studying the New Testament Use of the Old Testament*. Grand Rapids: Baker Academic, 2010.

Murphy, Roland E., and O. Carm. "Wisdom and Creation." *Journal of Biblical Literature* 104, no. 1(1985): 3-11.

O'Brien, Peter T. *Colossians, Philemon: 44 (Word Biblical Commentary)*. Nashville: Thomas Nelson, 1982.

Patzia, Arthur G. *Ephesians, Colossians, Philemon: New International Bible Commentary*. Peabody: Hendrickson, 2004.

Peng, Kuo-Wei. "Image Restored Through Christ: The Image of God in Pauline Epistles." *Living Pulpit (Online)* 22, no. 1(2013).

Peterson, Jeffrey. "The Image of God in Pauline Preaching." *Leaven* 16, no. 2: Creation and New Creation(2008).

Porter, Stanley E., ed. *The Messiah in the Old and New Testaments*. Grand Rapids: Eerdmans, 2007.

Sanders, E. P. *Paul: A Very Short Introduction*. Oxford: Oxford University Press, 2001.

—. *Paul and Palestinian Judaism: A Comparison of Patterns of Religion*. Philadelphia: Fortress Press, 1977.

Schreiner, Thomas R. "Paul: A Reformed Reading." Pages 19-47 in *Four Views on the Apostle Paul*. Edited by Michael F. Bird. Grand Rapids: Zondervan, 2012.

Schweizer, Eduard. *The Letter to the Colossians: A Commentary*. Minneapolis: Augsburg Press, 1982.

Smith, Mark S. *The Priestly Vision of Genesis 1*. Minneapolis: Fortress Press, 2010.

Stanley, Christopher D., ed. *Paul and Scripture: Extending the Conversation*. Atlanta: SBL, 2012.

Stendahl, Krister. *Paul Among Jews and Gentiles, and other essays*. London: SCM, 1977.

Stettler, Christian. "The Opponents at Colossae." Pages 169-200 in *Paul and his Opponents*. Edited by Stanley E. Porter. Leiden: Brill NV, 2005.

Sumney, Jerry L. "Writing "In The Image" Of Scripture: The Form And Function Of References To Scripture In Colossians." Pages 185-229 in *Paul and Scripture: Extending the Conversation*. Edited by Christopher D. Stanley. Atlanta: SBL, 2012.

Thiselton, Anthony C. *The Living Paul: An Introduction to the Apostle Life and His Thought*. London: Society for Promoting Christian Knowledge, 2009.

Thompson, James W. "Paul as Missionary Pastor." Pages 25-36 in *Paul as Missionary: Identity, Activity, Theology, and Practice*. Edited by Trevor J. Burke and Brian S. Rosner. London: T & T Clark, 2011.

Thompson, Marianne Meye. *Colossians and Philemon*. Grand Rapids: Eerdmans, 2005.

Bibliography

Thompson, Michael Bruce. *The New Perspective on Paul.* Grove Books, 2002.

Turner, Laurence A. *Genesis.* Sheffield: Sheffield Phoenix Press, 2009.

Van Kooten, George H. *Paul's Anthropology in Context.* Tubingen: Mohr Siebeck, 2008.

Van Wolde, Ellen. *Stories of the Beginning: Genesis 1-11 and Other Creation Stories.* Ridgefield: Morehouse Publishing, 1997.

Von Rad, Gerhard. *Genesis.* Philadelphia: SCM Press, 1972.

Wall, Robert W. *Colossians and Philemon (IVP New Testament Commentary).* Downers Grove: Inter Varsity Press, 1993.

Walsh, Brian J., and Sylvia C. Keesmaat. *Colossians Remixed: Subverting the Empire.* Downers Grove: Inter Varsity Press, 2004.

Weiss, Herold. "The Law in the Epistle to the Colossians." *Catholic Biblical Quarterly* 34, no. 3(1972): 294-314.

Wengst, Klaus. *Pax Romana and the Presence of Jesus Christ.* Translated by J. Bowden. London: SCM Press, 1987.

Wenham, David. *Paul: Follower of Jesus or Founder of Christianity?* Grand Rapids: Eerdmans, 1995.

Wenham, Gordon. *Genesis 1-15.* Nashville: Thomas Nelson, 1986.

—. "Grace and Law in the Old Testament." In *Law, Morality and the Bible*. Edited by Bruce Kaye and Gordon Wenham. Downers Grove: InterVarsity Press, 1978.

Westerholm, Stephen. *Perspectives Old and New in Paul: The "Lutheran" Paul and his Critics*. Grand Rapids: Eerdmans, 2004.

Westerman, Claus. *Blessing in the Bible and the Life of the Church*. Minneapolis: Fortress Press, 1978.

Worthington, Jonathan D. *Creation in Paul and Philo*. Tubingen: Mohr Siebeck, 2011.

Wright, N. T. *Colossians and Philemon: An Introduction and Commentary*. Nottingham: Inter-Varsity Press, 2008.

—. *Paul and the Faithfulness of God*. London: Society for Promoting Christian Knowledge, 2013.

—. *Paul: Fresh Perspectives*. London: SPCK, 2005.

—. "Paul's Gospel and Caesar's Empire." Pages 160-83 in *Paul and Politics: Ekklesia, Israel, Imperium, Interpretation: Essays in Honour of Krister Stendahl*. Edited by Richard A. Horsley. Harrisburgh: Trinity, 2000.

—. *The Climax of the Covenant: Christ and the Law in Pauline Theology*. Minneapolis: T & T Clark, 1993.

Wright, Tom. *What St Paul Really Said*. Oxford: Lion Publishing, 1997.

Bibliography

Zetterholm, Magnus. *Approaches to Paul: A Student's Guide to Recent Scholarship.* Minneapolis: Fortress, 2009.

Ziesler, John. *Pauline Christianity.* Oxford: Oxford University Press, 1983.

The Colossian Image

INDEX OF ANCIENT SOURCES

OLD TESTAMENT

Genesis

1	30, 66, 69, 97, 118, 120, 133, 134, 135, 143
1:1	9, 69
1:2	69
1:3	69, 125
1:20	128
1:24-30	124
1:24	124
1:26-27	26, 128, 138
1:26-28	29, 30, 34, 36, 37, 59, 69, 117, 118, 126, 135, 188, 193, 199
1:26	9, 127, 128, 130, 135, 194, 199
1:27	96, 125, 126, 135, 142, 143, 199
1:28	59, 128, 131, 135, 148, 199
2:7	70
2:15	53, 129
6:8	173
9:6	69
12:1-3	193
12:3	54
15	193
17	193
17:4-14	187
17:5-6	189
17:8	189
17:9-10	158
17:10-14	181
17:12	189
17:12-13	189
18:3	173
39:21	173
47:11	45

Exodus

3:6	176
3:8	68
3:19-22	69
3:21	173
4:22	53, 70
4:31	80
6:6	68
11:3	173
19:5-6	192, 193
19:6	45, 133
20:1-17	175, 192
20:2	53, 176
20:22-23:19	175
23:10-19	158
23:21	158, 163
24:7-8	173
24:7	173
33:13	173

Leviticus

11:1-23	158
11:24-45	158
11:45	176
16:1-34	174
19:2	45

19:36	176		18:1	129
25	129		24:6	176
25:38	176		24:14	181
26:12	178			
26:13	176			

Numbers

Judges

5:1-4	158		6:8	176
11:11	173		6:9	80
15:41	176		10:6-16	80
19:11	158			
32:5	173			

1 Samuel

32:22	129		10:18	176
32:29	129		26:23	181
33:52	132			
33:54	67, 111			

2 Samuel

			7:5-16	68
			10:18-19	80

Deuteronomy

1 Kings

4:20	67		12:28	176
4:29	80			
5:6	176			

2 Kings

5:33	165		11:18	132
10:9	67		17:36	176
10:12	111		19:3	80
10:16	181			
14:3-21	158			

1 Chronicles

24:1	173		11:9	53
28:47-68	80		16:13	192
30:6	173		23:31	158, 164
30:10	173			
30:15-20	181			
30:16	173			
32:6	53			

Joshua

1:6	111

Index of Ancient Sources

2 Chronicles

2:4	164
7:1-3	181
7:12	133, 181
8:13	164
23:17	132
28:10	129
31:3	164
36:22-23	69

Nehemiah

5:5	129
9:6	69
10:33	158, 164

Esther

7:8	129

Job

28:28	111

Psalms

72	129
81:10	176
86:6	173
105:6	192
105:43	192
106:5	192
130:4	111

Proverbs

8	34, 118
8:22-30	124
8:22-31	31, 96, 117
8:22	118
8:23	118, 120
8:24	118
8:27	117
8:29-30	117
8:30	118, 121

Isaiah

31:4-5	68
40:3	53
43:20	192
44:24	69
45:4	192
65:9	192
66:2	69

Jeremiah

3:9	53
3:18	111
11:4	176
23:7-8	68
31:2	173
31:31-34	189
31:31	181
32:21	176
34:11	129

Ezekiel

7:20	132
11:17-20	189
16:17	132
34	129
45:17	158, 164

Daniel		Amos	
1:3-16	164	2:10	176
1:8	158	3:1	45, 176
2:18-19	80	5:26	132
2:27-30	80		
10:3	164		

Micah	
2:3	45
2:4	111
4:10	68
6:4	176

Hosea	
2:11	158, 164

Zechariah	
12:10	173

APOCRYPHA

Wisdom of Solomon		Ben-Sirach	
2:23	124	17:3	124
4:15	192	24:4-5	124
7	34		
7:22	124		
7:26	31, 96, 119, 120		
8:6	124		

2 Esdras	
8:44	124

Index of Ancient Sources

PSEUDEPIGRAPHA

Aristeas, Letter of

142	158

2 Baruch

20	79
25	79

3 Baruch

12:3	113

1 Enoch

6:7-8	113
47:2-4	78
51:3	80
61:10	113
103:2	80

2 Enoch

20:1	113

3 Enoch

12:5	158

Testament of Abraham

13:10	113

Testament of Levi

3:8	113

Testament of Solomon

3:5	113
8:6	113

4 Ezra

4:12	79
4:33-37	79
4:33-43	78
4:36	78
13:16-19	79
14:5	80

NEW TESTAMENT

Matthew		6:56	149
		7:22	181
1:22	53	8:41	53
3:16	141	10:30	97, 149
5:17	164, 181	11:26	149
6:10	202	12:13	53
14:2	149	13:31	149
21:38	111	13:32	149
22:19	108	14:9	25, 97
22:20	95, 108	14:10	149
		14:11	149
Mark		14:20	149
		15:2	149
1:10	141	15:4	149
1:15	178	15:5	149
6:14	149	15:6	149
12:15	108	15:7	149
12:16	95, 108	16:33	149
		17:21	149
Luke		17:23	149
1:68	53	Acts	
3:22	141		
5:20-21	111	1:8	144
20:24	95, 108	3:22	53
21:26	111	7:53	163
22:17	149	17:28	25, 149
22:20	181, 189	18	164
23:22	149	18:21	176
23:34	111	22:25-29	105
		24:14	164, 176
John		25:8	164, 176
1:4	149	Romans	
1:14	69		
1:32-33	141	1:3	123

228

Index of Ancient Sources

1:7	44, 112	8:17	81
1:8	52	8:18	80
1:8f	49	8:29	10, 29, 81, 100, 150, 203
1:11-15	72		
2:10	112	8:38	113
2:13	179	8:39	150
2:14-15	179	9-11	188
2:25-29	179	9:1	150
3:17	112	9:28	111
3:20	174	9:29	53, 111
3:24	150, 172	9:33	149
3:31	164	10:4	163, 181
4:5	149, 150	10:11	149
4:8	111	10:14	149
4:15	100	10:16	111
4:16	172	11:3	111
4:17-19	100	11:6	172
4:24	150	11:34	111
5:1	112	12:2	137
5:1-5	56	12:5	150
5:3	80	12:11	111
5:12-21	139, 203	12:19	111
5:14	139	14:11	111
5:15-19	123	14:17	112
5:16	139	14:19	112
5:17	139	14:21	164
5:18	139	15:11	111
5:21	139	15:12	150
6:6	139	15:13	112
6:11	150	15:14-32	72
6:14	172	15:33	112
6:15	164	16:3	149
6:23	150	16:4	172
7:6	203	16:7	149
7:7	174	16:9	149
7:12	164, 171	16:10	149
7:22	164	16:20	112
8:1-2	150		
8:6	112		

1 Corinthians

1:2	44, 149, 150
1:4	52, 150
1:4f	49
1:5	150
1:24	100
1:30	24, 100, 149
2:2	77
3:1	150
4:10	150
4:17	149
5:7	203
8:8	179
9:20	176
11:25	45
12:3	142
13:13	56
15:18	150
15:22	150, 203
15:45-49	100, 139
15:45	203
15:49	10, 203
16:1-11	72

2 Corinthians

1:1	45
1:3	52
1:5-7	80
1:21	150
2:14	150
2:17	150
3:18	10, 81, 100, 203
4:4	10, 96, 100, 125, 203
4:6	125
4:16	137
4:17-18	80
5:17	203, 150
5:19	150
5:21	24, 150
7:4	80
8:9	24
9:8	176
12:2	149

Galatians

1:4	77
1:10-2:21	72
2:4	150
2:16-17	150
2:16	149
2:21	172
3:1	123
3:6-9	188
3:13-14	188
3:10-14	163
3:14	150
3:19	163, 174
3:23-26	163, 188
3:26	150
3:27-29	188
3:27	188
3:28	142, 188
4:4	123
5:2-6	179
5:4	172
5:5-6	57
5:22	59
6:15	203

Ephesians

1:1	45, 149
1:3	52, 150
1:4	150

Index of Ancient Sources

1:7	150	3:9	149, 150
1:10	150	3:10	81
1:11	150	3:14	150
1:13	149	3:20	110
1:15	57	4:19	150
1:15f	49	4:21	149
1:18	57		
1:21	77	**Colossians**	
2:2	113		
2:5	172	1:1-2	41
2:5-7	150	1:1	43, 56, 71
2:8-9	172, 175	1:2	43, 44, 45, 53, 84, 109, 149, 151, 168
2:10	150		
2:13-15	172	1:3-8	54
2:13	150	1:3-9	54, 55
2:15-16	112	1:3-12	49, 56, 75
2:15	100, 140, 203	1:3-2:23	22
2:16	112	1:3	50, 51, 52, 53, 54, 55, 56, 71, 100, 109
2:22	150		
3:6	150	1:4-5	198
3:12	149	1:4	54, 56, 62, 71, 149, 151, 168, 177, 178
4:2-5	57		
4:22-24	139		
4:24	203		
5:23	110	1:5	56, 109, 155
		1:6	54, 59, 109, 168
Philippians		1:7-8	43, 55, 71
		1:7	51, 56, 180
1:1	45, 149	1:8	56, 62, 71, 76, 141, 168
1:3	52		
1:3f	49	1:9-11	54, 57
1:12-26	72	1:9-12	54
1:26	149	1:9	54, 57, 58, 59, 62, 71
1:29	149		
2:6	100	1:10	54, 56, 58, 59, 109
2:7	123, 141		
2:9	123	1:11-12	50
2:9-11	100	1:11	58, 59, 141
3:3	149		

1:12	50, 54, 55, 61, 62, 67, 69, 171, 174		92, 99, 104, 118, 119, 120, 121, 123, 135, 152, 198, 199
1:13-14	21, 61, 62, 64, 66, 68, 100, 101, 102, 198	1:19	25, 76, 85, 86, 92, 103, 135, 141, 149, 151, 152, 153, 180, 181, 198
1:13-15	64		
1:13-20	61, 65, 66, 68, 101	1:20-23	70, 81, 198
		1:20	66, 91, 99, 102, 109, 152, 153, 155, 174
1:13-23	21, 61, 71, 147		
1:13	61, 62, 63, 64, 68, 69, 91, 102, 109	1:21-22	21
		1:21-23	62, 67
		1:21	63, 67
1:14	63, 68, 91, 102	1:22	82, 109, 177
1:15-16	70, 99, 162	1:23-2:5	51
1:15-17	99, 118, 151	1:23	71, 109, 177
1:15-20	26, 41, 51, 61, 62, 63, 66, 96, 98, 113, 117, 120, 135, 151, 152	1:24-25	72
		1:24-29	74
		1:24-2:5	43, 71, 74
1:15	10, 11, 21, 23, 25, 29, 30, 31, 63, 64, 69, 91, 92, 93, 96, 97, 98, 101, 104, 111, 113, 117, 118, 119, 120, 125, 126, 135, 138, 139, 195, 197, 199	1:24	30, 33, 72, 73, 75, 76, 79, 80, 81
		1:25	74
		1:26-27	72, 74
		1:26	75, 157
		1:27	42, 72, 73, 74, 75, 76, 77, 100, 147, 157, 162, 171
1:16-17	99	1:28-29	72
1:16	21, 23, 25, 69, 92, 96, 104, 109, 111, 113, 118, 125, 135, 151, 152, 198, 199	1:28	41, 47, 72, 74, 82, 86, 120, 135, 149, 150, 151
		1:29	72, 73, 75, 80
1:17-18	99	2:1-5	75
1:17	25, 91, 92, 104, 119, 135, 149, 150, 151, 153, 198, 199	2:1	43, 62, 72, 73, 75
		2:2-3	75, 147
		2:2-5	72
1:18-20	66, 99, 151	2:2	72, 73, 75, 81, 137, 157, 162
1:18	23, 25, 43, 70, 81,		

Index of Ancient Sources

2:3	81, 100, 120, 151		163, 174, 181, 184, 200
2:4-5	75		
2:5	62, 72, 73, 141, 149, 151, 168, 177	2:12-13	92, 198
		2:12	24, 25, 30, 43, 84, 86, 87, 100, 137, 151, 152, 155, 177, 180, 187, 198, 200
2:6-7	27, 151, 153, 184, 185		
2:6-11	76		
2:6-19	83, 84, 86, 87, 151, 152, 184, 186		
		2:13	84, 87, 123, 152, 157, 158, 181, 184
2:6-23	47, 151, 155, 158, 192	2:13-14	174, 180
2:6-4:1	46	2:14	152, 158, 163, 200
2:6-4:6	83	2:15	25, 87, 92, 109, 147, 149, 150, 151, 152, 162, 180, 184, 198, 199
2:6	25, 83, 84, 109, 137, 144, 145, 149, 151, 155, 165, 199		
		2:16-18	187
2:7	25, 50, 84, 149, 151, 155, 168, 177, 199	2:16-23	84
		2:16	152, 155, 157, 158, 163, 169, 174, 181, 185, 200
2:8	41, 43, 58, 84, 152, 155, 160, 161, 163, 169, 170, 181, 184, 185		
		2:17	163
		2:18	33, 152, 155, 157, 158, 159, 160, 169, 184, 185, 200
2:8-23	21, 42, 147		
2:9-10	85, 100, 147, 162		
2:9	25, 76, 84, 86, 141, 149, 151, 152, 155, 180, 181, 198	2:19	168, 169, 171, 185, 200
		2:20-22	163
2:10-12	198	2:20-23	161
2:10-14	151	2:20-3:4	83, 88, 89
2:10	25, 76, 84, 85, 87, 92, 149, 151, 152, 155, 162, 184, 187, 194, 198, 198, 199, 200	2:20	30, 137, 163
		2:21-22	181
		2:21	158
		2:23	120, 157
		3:1-4	22, 43, 84
2:11-13	62, 162	3:1-17	71
2:11	25, 84, 139, 149, 151, 155, 157, 158,	3:1-4:17	22
		3:1	22, 24, 30, 88, 92,

	100, 137, 147, 198	3:18-19	42
3:3	147	3:18-4:1	190, 198
3:4	92, 100	3:18	109, 190
3:5-9	84, 195	3:19	190
3:5-17	30, 88, 90, 187, 198	3:20-21	42
		3:20	109, 190
3:5-4:1	181, 190, 201	3:21	190
3:5-4:6	83	3:22	42, 109, 111, 190
3:5	192, 193	3:23	42, 109, 190
3:6	109, 187, 192	3:24	109, 111, 190
3:8	193	4:1	42, 109
3:9-10	90, 140, 154	4:2	50
3:9-11	23, 27, 28, 32, 191	4:3	43, 157
3:9	41, 44, 139, 140, 193, 195	4:5	120
		4:7	43, 109
3:10-11	195	4:9	43
3:10	10, 11, 23, 25, 81, 31, 41, 43, 44, 89, 92, 95, 97, 120, 137, 138, 139, 140, 142, 148, 155, 177, 188, 190, 194, 195, 197, 199, 201	4:10-11	42
		4:12	43, 51
		4:13	43
		4:14	43
		4:15	43
		4:16	43
		4:17	43, 109
3:11	39, 42, 92, 142, 188, 189, 198	**1 Thessalonians**	
3:12-17	43, 195		
3:12-4:1	84, 192	1:2f	49
3:12	187, 188, 192, 193, 195	1:2-3	52
		1:3	57
3:13-14	193	1:6	80
3:13	90, 91, 109, 111	2:15	123
3:14-15	92	2:17-3:11	72
3:14	92, 188, 198	5:8	57
3:15-17	100		
3:15	50, 90, 91, 109, 194	**2 Thessalonians**	
3:16	50, 90, 91, 92, 120, 162, 198	1:3	52
		1:3f	49
3:17	50, 90, 109, 194		

Index of Ancient Sources

1 Timothy

1:1	110
1:12f	49
1:14	150
1:16	149, 150
1:17	110
2:3	110
2:5	123
3:16	100
4:10	110
6:15	110
6:15-16	100

2 Timothy

1:1	149
1:3	52
1:3-7	49
1:9	150
1:10	110
1:13	150
2:1	150
2:10	150
3:15	149

Titus

1:3	110
1:4	110
2:3	100
2:10	110
2:13	110
3:4	110
3:6	110

Philemon

4	52
4f	49
21-22	72
23	149

Hebrews

1:8-9	100
2:17	100, 110
3:1	110
3:14	149
4:14	110
4:15	100, 110
5:1	110
5:5	110
5:10	110
6:10-12	57
6:20	110
7:26	110
7:27	110
7:28	110
8:1	110
8:3	110
9:7	110
9:11	110
10:22-24	57
11:13	68
13:11	110

1 Peter

1:1	68
1:3-8	57
1:17	68
1:21	57
1:22	57
2:9	133
2:11	68
3:16	149
3:22	113

5:10	149		3:5	149
5:14	149		3:6	149
			3:15	149
1 John			3:17	149
			3:24	149
1:5	149		4:13	149
2:4	149		4:15	149
2:5	149		4:16	149
2:6	149		5:20	149
2:8	149			
2:10	149		**Revelation**	
2:15	149			
2:27	149		4:8	53
2:28	149			

PHILO

De somnis			*De fuga et invention*	101
1.239	124, 125			
1.141-143	158		*De confusion linguarum*	97, 147
2.45	124			

EARLY CHRISTIAN TEXTS

Cave of treasures			**Athanasius**	
1:3	113		*Against the Arians*	
Justin Martyr			2.16.18-24	117
Dialogue			*On the incarnation of the Word*	
34.2	158			
			54.3	24

www.ingramcontent.com/pod-product-compliance
Lightning Source LLC
Chambersburg PA
CBHW020850090426
42736CB00008B/317